WRITE
TO THE TOP
Writing for Corporate
Success

WRITE TO THE TOP

Writing for Corporate Success

DEBORAH DUMAINE

RANDOM HOUSE
New York

Library of Congress Cataloging in Publication Data

Dumaine, Deborah.
Write to the top.

Bibliography: p.
1. Communication in management.   2. Commercial
correspondence.   I. Title.
HF5718.D84   658.4'53   82–40145
ISBN 0–394–71226–9   AACR2

Book design: Charlotte Staub

Manufactured in the United States of America
468975

*Dedicated
with love to
my family*

Acknowledgments

Many people gave me the support and advice that made this book possible. First I would like to acknowledge and thank Sherri Federbush for her assistance as developmental editor.

I would also like to thank Priscilla Claman, Brian Dumaine, Caroline Sutton, Harry Saxman and Susan Gill for their excellent editorial suggestions. Original ideas for work sheets and exercises came from Michael Segal, Ann Blum and, above all, my sister Miriam Dumaine, my mainstay during the entire project. Lisa Danchi was extremely helpful throughout, offering constructive criticism and devoted attention to the fine details of the manuscript. Thanks also go to Charlotte Mayerson, my editor, for her enthusiasm about this book.

Write to the Top reflects not only my efforts but the originality and expertise of the entire staff of seminar leaders at Better Communications. My most enormous thanks, therefore, go to them—for their droll camaraderie, for their constant interest in making our workshops the best possible and for their wonderful dedication:

Eve Goodman	*Alex Johnson*
Marea Gordett	*Carolyn Russell*
Karen Horowitz	*Jenny Webster*

Contents

Introduction   xi

PART ONE: Issues We All Face   1

1. Why Write?   3

2. Six Strategies for Getting Started   14
For All Types of Writing: The Traditional Outline   17
For Short Memos and Letters: The Start-Up Sheet   17
For Long Memos and Reports: The Brainstorm Outline   19
For Long Reports: Planning with Index Cards   28
For Long Memos and Reports: Post-It Note Tape   29
For All Types of Writing: Liberate Your Thoughts with Free Writing   30

3. The Right Look   34

4. Positioning Your Ideas: Choosing a Method of Development   46
Methods of Development for Organizing Letters, Memos and Reports   46
Method of Development #1: Order of Importance   47
Method of Development #2: Chronology   53
Method of Development #3: Sequence   53
Method of Development #4: Organization in Space   54
Method of Development #5: Comparison   54
Method of Development #6: Specific to General or General to Specific   55
Method of Development #7: Analysis   55
The Organization Game   57

5. Writing the First Draft 63
   When You're Stuck 67
   How to Write a Problem-Solving Memo 69

6. Writing to Persuade 73

7. Are You Communicating? 87
   Negotiations and Strategies 87
   Getting Action from Your Writing 90
   Abstract Obscurity 93
   Measuring the Readability Level of Your Writing 97
   How to Be a Dictator 99

PART TWO: Quiz Yourself 101

8. What Are Your Personal Strengths and Weaknesses? 103
   Dangling Modifiers 103
   Gobbledygook 105
   Streamlining 107
   The Active Voice 109
   Parallelism 111
   Consistency 112
   Making Logical Comparisons 114
   Pronoun Agreement 115
   Using Commas around Phrases 116
   Semicolons 118
   Colons 119
   Dashes 121
   Apostrophes 122
   Your Personal Profile 123

9. Be Your Own Editor 125
   The Spelling Cheat Sheet 127

   Appendix A: Solutions to Exercises 133

   Appendix B: Fry's Readability Graph 139

   Suggested Reading 141

Introduction

Good writing is a powerful tool: it can make your message stand out from the mass of writing competing for attention in corporations every day. It can distinguish your ideas, focus them for impact and help you get the response you want from your colleagues. If you can't write clearly and powerfully, your career advancement will always be seriously limited.

As business becomes more complex and the layers of management grow, so does the need for concise, clear writing. Whether you're writing a letter, a sales memo or a detailed financial report, it is crucial that it be brief, lucid and persuasive so that the particular significance of your thoughts and information can be easily grasped and used.

Executives don't have the time—or the inclination—to unravel confusing proposals or poorly organized and presented material. Even ideas that have genuine merit for the company and that would be valuable to your own career can be defeated by mediocre writing.

As a writer, corporate trainer, editor, reading specialist and faculty member at Simmons Graduate School of Management, I have spent the last five years developing writing improvement techniques specifically designed to meet the needs of the corporate writer. My company, Better Communications, has used these methods successfully to develop managers' skills in such major companies as Digital Corporation, Fidelity Management Research Corporation, Honeywell Incorporated, Wang Laboratories and New England Life Insurance Company. Through workshops and private counseling, my staff and I have taught managers and executives how to achieve a special edge in the competitive world of business by giving their ideas the proper form and expression. We've also assembled techniques and exercises for overcoming writer's block, modernizing style and increasing writing speed.

The Better Communications Method you will find in this book divides the writing task into a series of subskills. You can assess your own competence in each area as you go along and then follow the appropriate exercises, which are, incidentally, fun to do. Some of your skills may only need to be sharpened; others may require more serious attention. The on-site workshop we deliver to corporate clients is self-paced and individualized. The exercises in this book reflect the same approach.

Write to the Top is divided into two parts: the first deals with the problems of getting started, organizing ideas for impact, persuasion, tone and style. Part two helps you with more specific problems, such as sentence construction, word choice, usage and grammar—the issues you face when finalizing a piece of writing. Mini-quizzes before each exercise in part two will help you pinpoint your individual strengths and weaknesses.

Like most skills, writing is improved primarily by practice. This book offers both the practice and the guidance that can sharpen your writing ability and make this daily task less burdensome. The exercises in this book all work—but only if you do. You must get involved in order to learn. No one becomes a faster jogger simply by reading a book about jogging; neither will you improve your writing by reading a book or listening to a lecture. This book offers a tested program which asks that you *write* as well as read. Just as running laps improves your running, every page you actually work on will benefit your writing.

PART ONE

Issues We All Face

1
Why Write?

Is this you? Ike Antwright glances at his watch and then back to the blank page in front of him. The ticking of the wall clock grows louder, and a siren outside the window makes him lose his train of thought for the second time. The right words are just beyond his reach.

His mind wanders to the next day's appointments and to the movie he is going to see with Elaine that evening. His secretary's telephone brings his attention back to the empty sheet on his desk. He thinks, "I'm just not getting anywhere. I know pretty much what I want to say, but I can't bring myself to write it down. I want to hint to Jack that I know who made the calls to Honolulu during the office party. But how to phrase it in this memo so the whole office doesn't take it as an attack on Jack? I want each person to think the memo pertains to everyone equally." Ike gets up, straightens out the papers on his desk, and decides that a cup of black coffee will wake him up. "I think I'll just let it go until tomorrow."

Most of us will avoid writing if we can. Most of us have felt at one time or another the way this poor executive does. Whether it's writing a long report or a short memo, we all find ourselves staring at the blank page more than we'd care to admit. At those times, the process can seem so overwhelming that we will do anything to avoid putting pen to paper.

In the office there are many distractions: the phone rings, an associate drops by, or there's a nice, mechanical job to do. Here is a list of obstacles to writing mentioned by members of a recent business writing workshop I conducted:

- I need to clean my entire office before I can start writing.
- I can't find the time to do my job and write this proposal, too.
- The boss called a special meeting.

- I don't understand why Dick wants me to put this in writing.
- I can't write until I've clipped my fingernails.

Almost any other activity will take precedence over writing for those who dread beginning or who are embarrassed about their skills.

Our audiovisual environment is encouraging poor writing skills. Telephones and television now make it possible to communicate with a minimum of reading or writing. Television connects us with news, entertainment and information. Telephones transmit messages quickly and easily over great distances. Computerized communications and teleconferences are already a reality.

People read dramatically fewer books than they did fifty years ago, as the struggling publishing industry demonstrates. With our diminishing reliance on letters and literature, we are becoming far less comfortable with the written word. No wonder many people say writing is the part of their job they like the least. In fact, most would probably be thrilled to see other methods of communication replace their writing responsibilities completely.

Why writing will always be a vital skill. Although technology can be cited as the cause for our ailing writing skills, writing will never go out of fashion. It may be possible for nonwriters to survive as passive receptors of the broadcasts of the audiovisual world, but those who wish to manipulate the technology—in other words, to have real power—will always turn to the written word as the starting point for thought transmission. Whether this writing appears on a display screen or a piece of paper is irrelevant.

A recent article about business schools in *Time* magazine stressed that graduates with good writing skills were in highest demand by corporate employers. Excellent writing correlates highly with the ability to think well—to analyze, weigh and decide. Another article, in the *Harvard Business Review,* listed writing ability as one of the crucial skills possessed by those who reach the top strata of corporate success. No one gets to the *very* top without being able to write well.

Why is writing so necessary? Most information is simply too complex for oral communication alone. Without writing as an aid to memory and understanding, the more sophisticated levels of thought are difficult to consider, much less document. Writing is thought on paper—our elusive ideas made real before us. It is the way most civilizations pass down knowledge for others to build upon. In the future, whatever messages flash on screens before our eyes won't have been written by robots, but by people skilled in clear writing.

Writing versus speaking. Everyone complains about the memo-maniac who floods peoples' in-boxes with unnecessary, unimportant memos. However, most of us have the opposite problem: we rely too much on the verbal. If an issue is fairly complex—if it includes pros and cons, solutions, explanations or implications—a memo may be needed. One important reason is this: if your audience receives your ideas in spoken form only, they are less likely to see things the way *you* do. Some people hear only what they want to hear; they fasten on the aspects that appeal to them and dismiss others even though they were discussed. In some situations, people simply do not hear correctly.

For example, when Justin Thyme wanted two of his assembly-line packers to work overtime to meet a crucial deadline, he thought he made them this verbal offer: "If you folks will work two hours overtime on Thursday and Friday plus come in for four hours on Sunday afternoon, you may take the following Monday off." To his dismay the packers, having put in their four hours' overtime, did not show up on Sunday, and all took Monday off anyway! This caused a whole new setback. When confronted about the confusion, the workers said they honestly hadn't heard Justin mention his need for them on Sunday. Had there been a loud, distracting noise as he spoke or had he himself forgotten to mention it? An expensive lesson in any case. Putting your information on paper will force people to consider your ideas carefully. They can't avoid them—your message is right before their eyes.

Meeting the needs of "visual" people. Cognitive studies show that some of us *must* have visual material in front of us in order to understand best. If your goal is to convince, you will double your impact if your proposal is on paper as well as spoken.

Unlike most oral presentations, a piece of writing can be most carefully planned and polished in advance. The perfect words and order of ideas can be chosen so that vital information appears at greatest advantage. Properly ordered ideas can make a great difference in a persuasive report. And once you are finished, all your information is there—nothing vital is lost. You are, if you want to be, on record. Your ideas can be considered and studied.

When is it better to write? Whatever business you're in, there are countless situations in which the visual effect of a written document is the best approach. (See "Negotiations and Strategies" in chapter 7.) A few are listed below. The first three combine both writing and speaking for a stronger result. The following three involve documents that stand on their own.

Persuasive proposals keep meetings on target. Consider this situation:

Hope Striver, recently hired at Polytrix, has developed an original new way to determine which promising managers should be promoted. It is a scheme based not only on past achievement but also on an assessment scale she developed that tests potential and native ability. She has named the scale "The Striver Management Promotion Scale." As you can imagine, many older managers will feel threatened by this plan.

Her written proposal explains the benefits of adopting the scale and then seeks to reassure those who might dislike it. At the meeting, Hope has a copy of the report for everyone. It forms the agenda for the meeting that she is leading. Because Hope put her most appealing arguments at the beginning of the report, many of the decision makers are influenced early in the meeting. Hope is able to hold off interruptions and objections until later by sticking to the order of ideas in the proposal. Those who disagree are given a fair hearing, but at a time when their views have less impact. In the end, Hope's carefully researched and ordered proposal, which seems even-handed in considering the needs of all involved, is accepted. Her initial work pays off. The proposal presented all the facts, yet it persuaded everyone of her point of view. Here is her informal outline of the proposal.

THE STRIVER MANAGEMENT PROMOTION SCALE

(1) Statement of introduction and recommendation
(2) Benefits
    a. Pinpointing people on the fast track
    b. Discouraging turnover
    c. Recognizing and rewarding talent and effort
(3) Calming fears
    a. No one will be demoted
    b. Certain people *will* be promoted more quickly
(4) How the scale works
(5) Who will be assessed
(6) Timetable for implementation
(7) Relation of the program to current career development program
(8) How the scale was developed: research and statistics
(9) Some unsuccessful past efforts of this nature

Let's consider what would have happened if Hope had entered the meeting room without having put her proposal on paper. Imagine the reaction of senior managers to the newcomer, Hope Striver, if she had opened the meeting with words like these: "I'm here to tell you about my new management promotion plan."

Cold suspicion might have filled the room. No report or agenda would have been available for participants to scan. It's not likely that the benefits of Hope's initiative would have occurred to most of those in attendance. Their first thoughts would probably have centered on their own job security. Without knowing that Hope had some weighty "persuaders" in mind, they could have started raising objections after five minutes—if she had gotten that far in her presentation. The meeting could easily have turned into Hope's baptism by fire as a new employee at Polytrix.

And you can guess how the meeting would have ended. Some cool-headed, experienced manager would have made the suggestion that Hope go back to the drawing board and prepare a written report for consideration at a later date. Much later.

Initial sales contacts. In a sales situation, the telephone may be an asset, but it is frequently the introductory *letter* that paves the way. The letter must be fairly brief while still covering the important selling points. You are in control of the subtle shades in tone and the right personal nuances. If you are a competent and cordial writer, you are more likely to find your way into someone's heart—and office—than if you introduce yourself point-blank on the phone. The chances of reaching a stranger by telephone are never great. Yet a well-written, professional-looking letter will make it into the in-box. Once it reaches the right hands, you have made an impression. Now you are ready to call—and very likely get through.

A letter like the one on page 8 opens doors.

Complaints. When you are telephoning with a complaint, you will probably have trouble getting through to the right person. You may have to call more than once to reach the person, or you may be left hanging "on hold" for what seems like ages. A letter will be much more effective. Direct it to the person who is really in charge and state your situation diplomatically but firmly. Acknowledge your faith in the company's desire for quality and good customer relations. In this way you are pushing just enough to get a response—chances are, a positive one—but not too hard.

An internal company complaint may also be treated in a similar way. State your problem, but offer the reader a way out—that is, a number of well-thought-out suggestions that show you are concerned enough to help find a solution. This gives the reader the time to see your point of view before a follow-up conversation.

On page 9 is an example of a successful letter of complaint. You can use it as a model for your own.

Recognizing achievements. One of the assistant managers in your insurance company has done an excellent job. How do you give him the reward he deserves?

A spoken compliment may be flattering, but a *letter* will have more impact

```
                        Quortle Graphic Design, Inc.
                        327 Tryon Avenue, Suite 5
                        San Francisco, CA

                        September 7, 1983

Mr. Al Bealright
Vice-President for Public Information
Intertrix
24 Lawton Street
San Francisco, CA

RE: Our wish to design your next brochure

Dear Mr. Bealright:

You people must be doing something right! The talk "on the
street" is that you're soon to go public with a new product
line that could seriously cut into your competition.

As the leading graphic design firm for your industry, we'd
be glad to meet with you to discuss design and production
prospects for the brochure you'll eventually need to help
promote your new product.

I've enclosed some examples of work we've done, a few of
which, I'm proud to say, have won us awards. We'd like to
have the opportunity to apply the same standards of
excellence for your firm on this very important project.

I'll wait until you've had a chance to look over our
materials before calling you. I hope we can meet to discuss
this project.


Cordially,


Art Graff
President


AG:sm
```

June 21, 1982

Mr. Justin Thyme
Manager, Customer Service
The Xolotl Corporation
5 Sumerlin Way
Schenectady, NY 30421

Re: Our need for a Service Rep *soon*

Dear Justin:

One of the reasons we bought Xolotl data processing
equipment was your reputation for providing good service.
Everyone we checked with rated you highly. Has something
changed?

I've been trying to get your service representative in
here for two weeks to have a look at our disc system. A
problem with the tape drive is occasionally damaging our
tapes.

If your service reps are too busy, we could bring in an
outside service group and send you the bill. I'd hate to do
this, but if we don't have it fixed by July 1, we'll have no
other choice.

I'm sure this problem is just the result of an oversight
that can be quickly remedied. Thank you in advance for
taking care of it. We look forward to a mutually helpful
working relationship.

Sincerely,

Anna Lyst
Systems Manager

AL/ss

November 14, 1983

Mr. Paul Penn
Publications Coordinator
Bingo Insurance Company
1229 Camel Drive
Miami, Florida 03672

Dear Paul,

Before you leave on your much-deserved vacation, I want to
tell you how much I appreciate your fine job of coordinat-
ing production of our annual report.

Not only is this year's model our most attractive and
best-packaged, it is also the most informative and
readable report in the history of our company.

I am deeply impressed with your efforts and will make
certain that your singular accomplishment is pointed out
to other members of the company.

If everyone here in the central office worked up to your
standards of efficiency and attention to detail, we'd set
a company-wide example of productivity that would be the
envy of the insurance industry.

Again, my congratulations on a job very well done.

Sincerely,

Lynn Thompson
Vice-President
Public Relations Department

LS:dc

cc: Carl Drake, Vice-President for Finance
    David Jeffreys, Vice-President for Public Information
    Cynthia Hyatt, Personnel Records Division

because it can be read by as many people as receive copies. The individual will always have that document as testimony to his or her success. As the superior, you will be able to distribute the letter to your colleagues to demonstrate the quality of work in your particular area. You will also be bringing your colleagues up to date on the activities of your division. A letter may take a bit more effort than verbal praise, but it has a more far-reaching effect.

Consider the one on page 10.

C.Y.A. Now imagine another situation, this time in a computer company:

Tom, a division manager responsible for keeping track of sales, is concerned that one of his salespeople, Herb, is not performing well. He has observed that he is in fact hurting the company's sales and image, but the upper-level executives have ignored his recommendations to let Herb go. Because he is not in the position to hire or fire, Tom must put his opinion, and what he has tried to do about the situation, in writing. This is commonly known in the business world as *covering your "anterior."* The document will protect the person when what he has predicted *will* happen does. If the boss starts pointing her finger, the writer has already taken himself off the hook.

Look at the memo on page 12.

News, changes and surprises. People often need time to digest news, whether it is good or bad. A written memo or report gives them that time. It says everything you would say yourself, but is more likely to be organized and authoritative. Readers will take it at their own pace, pausing when necessary and continuing when ready.

It is impossible to deal with each member of a large corporation for personal explanations of a policy change. A written memo easily reaches every employee and explains the news in as much detail as you want. Writing also allows you to plan your words and so create the effect you desire. It gives readers a chance to think about and adjust to news before giving their responses.

In the following example, a memo helped workers at Creemytrix to accept a potentially upsetting policy change. When Rick Cotta took over the manufacturing arm of a small yogurt company, he found it hard to tell his workers that a time clock was being installed—everyone would now have to punch in and out. By sending a clear and caring memo that emphasized the benefits of the new policy, he succeeded (see page 13).

So, are you ready to begin? It's easy to know *when* to write. The challenge is knowing *how* to write, especially how to begin.

In the next chapter you will find some strategies for helping you pull your thoughts together even when you're not quite sure what you want to say. Some of the devices are new ideas, others have been used successfully for years. Each strategy has proved to be a lifesaver for those who attend our workshops and who have trouble with the very beginning phase of the writing process. In every workshop, at least one of these strategies has transformed a despairing writer to a born-again writer, undaunted by the next memo deadline.

MEMORANDUM

TO: Jane Watson, Vice-President for Sales

FROM: Tom Narr, Director of Sales Management Development

RE: Sales Force performance update: good news and bad news

I have just completed the most recent quarterly report on sales force performance and want to pass along a few preliminary findings to you. A formal report will follow in three weeks.

A Problem in the Sales Team
For the third consecutive quarter, our team's sales figures look good, but there is one exception: Herb Gladhand. Aside from Herb, our entire sales team either met or exceeded individual quotas set at the beginning of the year.

As we all know, Herb refuses to part with his squirt-you-in-the-face lapel daisy despite warnings from all sides that this type of sales technique went out of style decades ago.

Action Taken
I have had several meetings with Herb to discuss ways in which his sales techniques might be modernized, all to no avail. In addition, I have brought this delicate matter to the attention of others in the firm, but they seem content with the overall figures and do not want to get involved with this personnel issue.

Recommendation
I firmly believe that more suitable work should be found for Herb, or that he should be replaced in order to improve our aggregate sales figures. If we don't take action on this soon I feel we could lag seriously in next quarter's performance figures.

TO: All yogurt manufacturing unit personnel
FROM: Rick Cotta
DATE: April 21, 1984
RE: New personnel policies

Background
For some time now here at Creemytrix, both management and
manufacturing personnel have suggested that work time
should be more efficiently and flexibly scheduled.
Management has been concerned that it does not have an
adequate method of determining who works when. And
manufacturing personnel have complained that the current
work schedule does not take into account the personal
needs of workers.

These schedules worked for us four years ago, when we were
smaller, but with our recent growth it's time for a change.
Several meetings have been held over the past few months,
and the following plans have been adopted.

Flextime
Starting next month, each person in the manufacturing unit
will be able to determine his or her own work week schedule
within certain guidelines. (See attached list of
acceptable work hours.) If a worker wishes to start and
complete the workday earlier, that will now be possible.
Conversely, the workday may start and end later. Also, it
will be possible to "get a jump on the weekend" by leaving
earlier on Friday if the weekly work has been completed.

Keeping track of hours
To keep track of hours worked each week, a time clock will
be installed in the manufacturing unit. Punching in will
take some getting used to, but after the initial and
anticipated confusion, the system should run smoothly.

Meeting to be announced
In a few days, I will announce the date and time of a
meeting to cover how the time clock arrangement will work.
Please be prepared to discuss any and all concerns you may
have. As soon as we iron out the kinks, the flextime policy
can be put into effect. This new system should make the
work week proceed more smoothly for all of us.

2
Six Strategies for Getting Started

Nobody needs convincing that getting started is for most of us the hardest part of writing—and especially of business writing. But it need not be such a distasteful chore. I have found that the Better Communications Start-Up materials, presented next, give managers a much more positive attitude toward the beginning phases of the writing task. With my step-by-step suggestions, your confidence will improve because you will have a method for attacking your writing that works. The first key to being a good writer is this: you must know what you want to say.

Developing your ideas. Any piece of writing over three paragraphs long requires planning: knowing your audience, your reason for writing, and, knowing generally what you want to say. In a three-paragraph memo, planning may consist of simply listing your three ideas in the order you'll present them. In longer documents, of course, developing your ideas takes more time. You may have to do serious research, go to the library, interview colleagues, speak to consultants, amass and analyze data from the computer. In any case you must list all of your ideas on paper so that you can (1) decide whether you really want to include them and (2) choose the best order in which to present them. As you will see, an entire chapter of this book has been devoted to the latter task.

Knowing exactly how much information you need to present isn't always easy, either. It takes as much skill to decide what to omit as what to include. One helpful guideline is this: less is more. Make your writing as brief as possible. Another good rule is to care more about protecting your readers than protecting yourself. Do whatever you can to save your readers from the mass of writing they confront daily.

Planning your time. Expect to spend most of your time developing your ideas and getting started. Ike Antwright had the bad habit of sitting down to write a first draft before planning his ideas. But bad habits like this one are time-consuming. In this book, as you'll see, writing the first draft isn't even considered until we are almost one-third through the program.

Be willing to put in the work preliminary to writing the first draft. It will make the actual writing faster and easier when you do get there. Remember, pencil-pushing is only a small part of writing. Here's my breakdown of how you should allocate your time.

5%	Know your objective: Action desired? Tone? Conclusion?
5%	Know your audience
25%	RESEARCH THE TOPIC Gather all facts Write out personal comments and interpretations Use a Start-Up Strategy if appropriate
15%	Organize information Analyze the facts Categorize with headlines
5%	Choose a Method of Development (M.O.D.): an order in which to present information
20%	Write a fast first draft
10%	Revise Have it typed
10%	Revise again Have it retyped
5%	Proofread

(Leftmost label, running vertically: YOUR TIME)

Choosing a Start-Up Strategy. Take a look at the Blank Page Syndrome chart below. There you will find some of the most common "symptoms" of writer's block among the managers I work with. It's a safe guess that some of these symptoms will be familiar to you.

Do you recognize any of them as your own? If so, find the appropriate remedy in the pages that follow.

Match the strategy to the task. Obviously, different writing tasks require different Start-Up techniques. For a short letter you may need only a mental plan or a quick list. A long report almost always requires extensive planning. Begin with the simplest situation—a short letter or a memo—and after you've mastered that, move on to more elaborate reports and proposals. Remember: difficult as it is for most people to conquer the blank page, things flow a lot more smoothly after planning with one of the following Start-Up Strategies.

THE BLANK PAGE SYNDROME
or Choosing the Right Start-Up Strategy

SYMPTOM	REMEDY
• You just don't know where to start.	For letters and short memos, try the *Start-Up Sheet*
	OR
	Use *Free Writing.* Just start writing and don't stop until all your ideas are on paper. Let yourself free-associate. Edit later.
• You need to organize and convey a large amount of information and over-look nothing.	Use the *Brainstorm Outline* format. Then number areas in logical order to create your particular outline,
	OR
	Use *Index Cards.* List ideas and data on cards, then organize,
	OR
	Organize with *Post-It Note Tape.* Put all of your notes on tape, then arrange them in order to create an outline.
• You're agonizing over your first draft, trying to make it perfect.	Use the *Free Writing* approach. (see above)
• You know exactly what you want to say and have a clear plan in mind.	Use the traditional outline.

FOR ALL TYPES OF WRITING: The Traditional Outline

What about the good old-fashioned outline? The idea of making a traditional outline filled Ike Antwright with dread. The mere mention of the word usually evoked a series of painful memories from college writing classes. Instead of helping him achieve his goal, the outline itself became a gruesome task. He remembered how his fat English professor, Mrs. Culpepper, directed him to make an outline before he wrote every paper. He would agonize over that outline for days. And when he wrote his paper without making an outline Mrs. Culpepper would inevitably say, "I want to see your outline." Then he would spend endless hours adjusting A's and B's, I's and II's, and 1, 2 and 3's.

In fact, he was afraid to outline because he wasn't yet sure what he wanted to say. He knew that an outline is the result of much thought and research. He just didn't know how to get to the point of being *ready* to make an outline.

Does Ike's predicament sound familiar? Remember, an outline is simply a list of ideas you want to include in your writing—arranged in a coherent order. If you can generate a "quick and dirty" list/outline, you don't need any other Start-Up Strategies; you're ready to start writing.

The five other strategies offered here are in fact pre-outline techniques to bring you to the final outline stage. They are all designed to spark a group of ideas you can then put in the best order (see chapter 4). Whether you wish to take these ideas one step further by copying them into outline form is up to you. If you do so, remember to indicate in some way the difference between main ideas and sub-ideas.

Here are a few ways to do that:

(1) Write main ideas in one color and less important ideas in a contrasting color. Use three colors if the list/outline is very complex.
(2) Mark main ideas with a special sign, such as a circle (or bullet), a star or an X. (· ★ X)
(3) Use A's and B's contrasted by Roman numerals—the traditional approach.

On page 18 is a sample outline for a proposal to purchase a word processor.

FOR SHORT MEMOS & LETTERS: The Start-Up Sheet

The Start-Up Sheet is a brief questionnaire that will help you pull your ideas together before you begin writing. By answering the series of questions it asks, you will find yourself assembling, step-by-step, your important points and facts. The Start-Up Sheet is particularly helpful for short tasks but can also start your thinking for long memos or reports.

TO PROPOSE PURCHASE OF A WORD PROCESSOR

   I. Overview

  II. The recommendation explained

     A. Benefits
       1. Saves time
       2. Saves money
       3. Makes perfect copies
       4. More creative use of personnel
         a. No need to hire a new typist
         b. Stores information

 III. Experiences of other users

     A. Company X
     B. Company Y
     C. Company Z

  IV. Background

     A. Other investigations on this issue
     B. Current equipment on hand

   V. Potential vendors

     A. Ace
     B. Acme
     C. Apex

  VI. Costs

     A. Financing
     B. The equipment
     C. Installation
     D. Training of personnel

 VII. Implementation timetable

     A. Space allocation
     B. Installation schedule
     C. Training schedule (personnel)

VIII. Long-term plans

     A. Options to upgrade
     B. Potential applications

  IX. Summary

How to use the Start-Up Sheet. Photocopy the Start-Up Sheet shown on pages 20–21. Many of the graduates of Better Communications workshops keep ten copies in their desks at all times—ready for action.

Let's go through the Start-Up Sheet, beginning with Step One, "Why are you writing this?" This is the fundamental question. If you can't answer the all-important *why* question, then you're in danger of writing a memo asking for a decision when you really mean to write a memo announcing a meeting at which the decision should be discussed. Jot down responses to the question *why?* until you're comfortable with your answer.

Step Two deals with your audience. Have you ever read a memo and thought to yourself, "Was this meant for me?" More likely than not, the memo writer got a little confused about who was supposed to be on the receiving end. You can cut down on paper, save people the trouble of sifting through inessential information, and possibly avoid embarrassment by keeping your reader in mind as you write.

At Step Three you must again focus on your goal for writing. Is your objective in sharp focus? Do you know what results you want to get? What do you expect people to *do* after reading your memo? Write as much as you need to answer this question; use extra paper if necessary. Your brainstorm answer could develop into the core paragraph of your memo or letter.

If you're having trouble answering the first three questions, you're not ready to write at all. Rethink the issues, research the answers, or ask colleagues who may know.

At Step Four, create your own questions, which your memo or letter will then answer. After you have filled in the sheet, rank your ideas as you want to present them in the memo or letter. You can copy them into outline form if you wish.

The value of the Start-Up Sheet will become apparent immediately. It creates a framework for your writing and saves time by helping you focus on the facts. Use Start-Up sheets every time you need help beginning a memo or letter.

ON YOUR OWN: Using the Start-Up Sheet as a planning guide, write a letter suggesting that a co-worker be given your company's award for most productive employee.

FOR LONG MEMOS & REPORTS:
The Brainstorm Outline

"How can I possibly keep track of all these ideas?" If you're writing a short memo or letter, the Start-Up Sheet will lead directly to the first draft. But if you're faced with a longer memo or a report, the Start-Up Sheet may not be enough. You need a way to get your ideas down before organizing them.

START-UP SHEET
MEMOS AND LETTERS

1. Why are you writing this?

   _____

   (This should give you your first sentence and arouse the reader's interest.)

2. Who will be reading it?

   _____

   (Keep this person in mind as you write.)

3. Answer the question below that seems most relevant to your memo. *(Check relevant box.)*

   ☐ What conclusion do you want the reader to reach?   or

   ☐ What is the problem you want to discuss?   or

   ☐ What is your position on the issue you are discussing?
   _____

   (Ideas from this line must be mentioned in the first paragraph if possible. If these are similar to question 1, don't worry.)

4. Now create your own questions relating to background, reasons, examples and supporting data, and list them below. See "The Most Commonly Used Headlines," in chapter 3, for inspiration. These are the questions you want to answer in your writing.

   (a) _____

   (b) _____

   (c) _____

   (d) _____

5. Sometimes you have ideas that don't seem to fit in anywhere. List these below. Use more paper if necessary.

   (a) _____

   (b) _____

6. Number the items in 4 and 5 in a sensible order.

(1) _____ (3) _____ (5) _____

(2) _____ (4) _____ (6) _____

7. Recap your main point at the end; consider adding a personal touch.

8. If you like, copy all the ideas from this sheet into a list-outline. Now you're ready to write!

This is how Ike Antwright used the Start-Up Sheet:

START-UP SHEET
MEMOS AND LETTERS

1. Why are you writing this?

To report on search for an in-state location for plant expansion.

(This should give you your first sentence and arouse the reader's interest.)

2. Who will be reading it?

Vice-president for facilities and operations, chief executive officer, and

(Keep this person in mind as you write.)   _possibly the board of directors._

3. Answer the question below that seems most relevant to your memo. *(Check relevant box.)*

   ☐ What conclusion do you want the reader to reach?   or
   ☑ What is the problem you want to discuss?   or
   ☐ What is your position on the issue you are discussing?

The company should expand its search and consider locating the new facility out-of-state

(Ideas from this line must be mentioned in the first paragraph if possible. If these are similar to question 1, don't worry.)

4. Now create your own questions relating to background, reasons, examples and supporting data, and list them below. See "The Most Commonly Used Headlines," in chapter 3, for inspiration. These are the questions you want to answer in your writing.

   (a) _Will cities be able to provide necessary support systems in the face of recently passed property tax limitation law?_

   (b) _Will limitation law be amended?_

   (c) _Is cost of living and cost of doing business too high in-state relative to other states?_

   (d) _Does the benefit of doing business in close proximity to central office outweigh higher costs of expanding here?_

5. Sometimes you have ideas that don't seem to fit in anywhere. List these below. Use more paper if necessary.

(a) *Will company founder and C.E.O. want to travel to new plant if it's located out-of-state?*

(b) *Do we have good enough relations with state officials, especially the governor, to attempt a little jaw-boning in our behalf to get access roads and the like built for us?*

6. Number the items in 4 and 5 in a sensible order.

(1) _4a_   (3) _4b_   (5) _4d_

(2) _5b_   (4) _4c_   (6) _5a_

7. Recap your main point at the end; consider adding a personal touch.

In my opinion, we should immediately begin to explore the prospects of opening our next facility out-of-state. After 7 weeks of interviews with state and local development officials, I believe that we are one year from being able to seriously consider an expansion here. It would take us at least that amount of time to explore out-of-state options, so we have nothing to lose. I would be happy to undertake the out-of-state search.

8. If you like, copy all the ideas from this sheet into a list-outline. Now you're ready to write!

The Brainstorm Outline allows you to pour out all your ideas without committing yourself in advance as to their relative importance or to the order in which you will ultimately present them. After you have mapped your ideas on the Brainstorm Outline, it is far easier to move on to an outline, if you like. If you find yourself thinking, "I have so many ideas, I just don't know how to begin," the Brainstorm Outline is for you.

What is a Brainstorm Outline? A Brainstorm Outline is a nonlinear, pictorial way of getting your ideas and their relationship to each other on paper. The Brainstorm Outline goes beyond the traditional outline because it opens you up to a very spontaneous way of thinking. It is especially helpful for writing problem-solving memos because it encourages free association—and provides lots of space on the outline for squeezing in new ideas. With this strategy, all your ideas are displayed at once, so you can easily see their relation to each other. Similar thoughts are grouped together. After you have completed the outline, you can then decide which ideas are most important by numbering them in the order you want to discuss them. If you like, you can copy them later into an easy-to-follow list or outline.

On page 25 is a sample Brainstorm Outline for a memo requesting the purchase of a word processor.

How to plan a report or memo using a Brainstorm Outline. First you will put all of your ideas down on paper in front of you so you can at least look at them. Those great ideas you have in the shower, when driving to work or before falling asleep can be forgotten or discounted until they are on paper. In fact, all the Start-Up Strategies are aimed at making sure you store your ideas, not in your head, but on paper, where they belong.

In the center of a large piece of plain white paper (minimum size: 8½″ × 11″) draw a circle big enough to contain six or seven words. In the circle, write the main goal of your memo or report. This will probably begin with a phrase such as:

to persuade   to analyze   to explain
to report findings   to request

Now draw a line extending out like the spoke of a wheel in any direction from the circle. As close as possible to the line, jot down an important idea that you want to include in your writing. It doesn't matter whether this is the idea you want to mention first or last in the final draft. Group ideas about the same subject along the same spoke or one emerging from it. List all ideas as they occur to you, as quickly as you can. Try to keep the momentum going. The Brainstorm Outline will look like a wheel with many spokes.

Continue adding more spokes for different thoughts. As you write each idea, ask yourself whether it deserves a new spoke of its own or whether it should be an offshoot of an already existing spoke.

THE BRAINSTORM OUTLINE

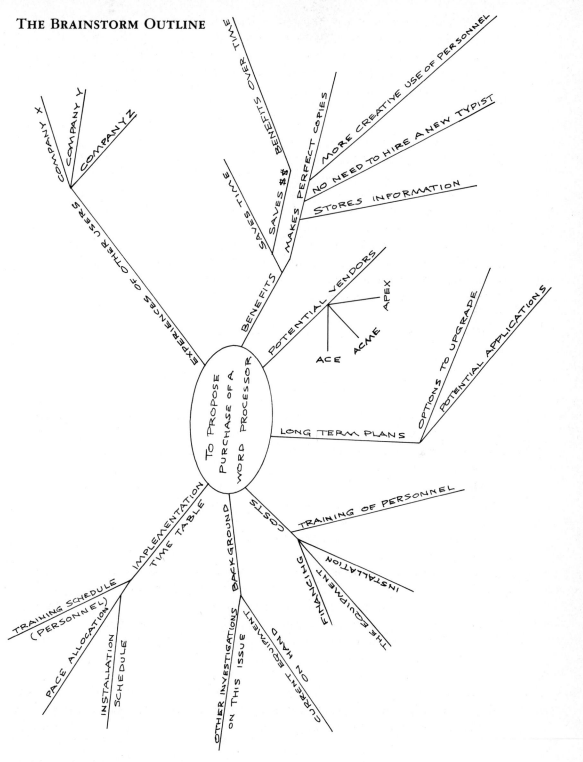

When all your thoughts are on the outline somewhere, you can begin to choose an order for presenting them in the actual memo. Number the spokes in the order that seems best (see chapter 4). When a group of words seems to hang together as one section, you can circle that area and put a number within the circle. If the outline is quite complex, you may want to circle numbered areas in different-colored inks.

Remember: (1) Put ideas that are related on the same spoke or close to it.

(2) Let the less important facts stem out of the most important ones.

(3) Rank your ideas after you have written them all down.

Now number the items in the sample brainstorm outline in the order you feel is most effective. If a group of words seems to hang together as one section, circle that area and put a number within the circle.

Page 27 shows how I ordered my ideas on this Brainstorm Outline.

Note: There can be more than one correct solution.

Using the Brainstorm Outline below, plan a memo suggesting a change in one of your company procedures which you believe would improve your working atmosphere.

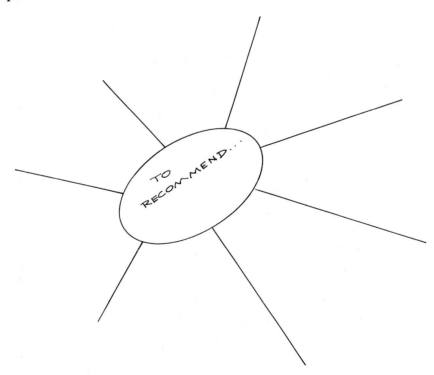

 ON YOUR OWN: Try using a Brainstorm Outline to plan your next memo or letter.

The Brainstorm Outline

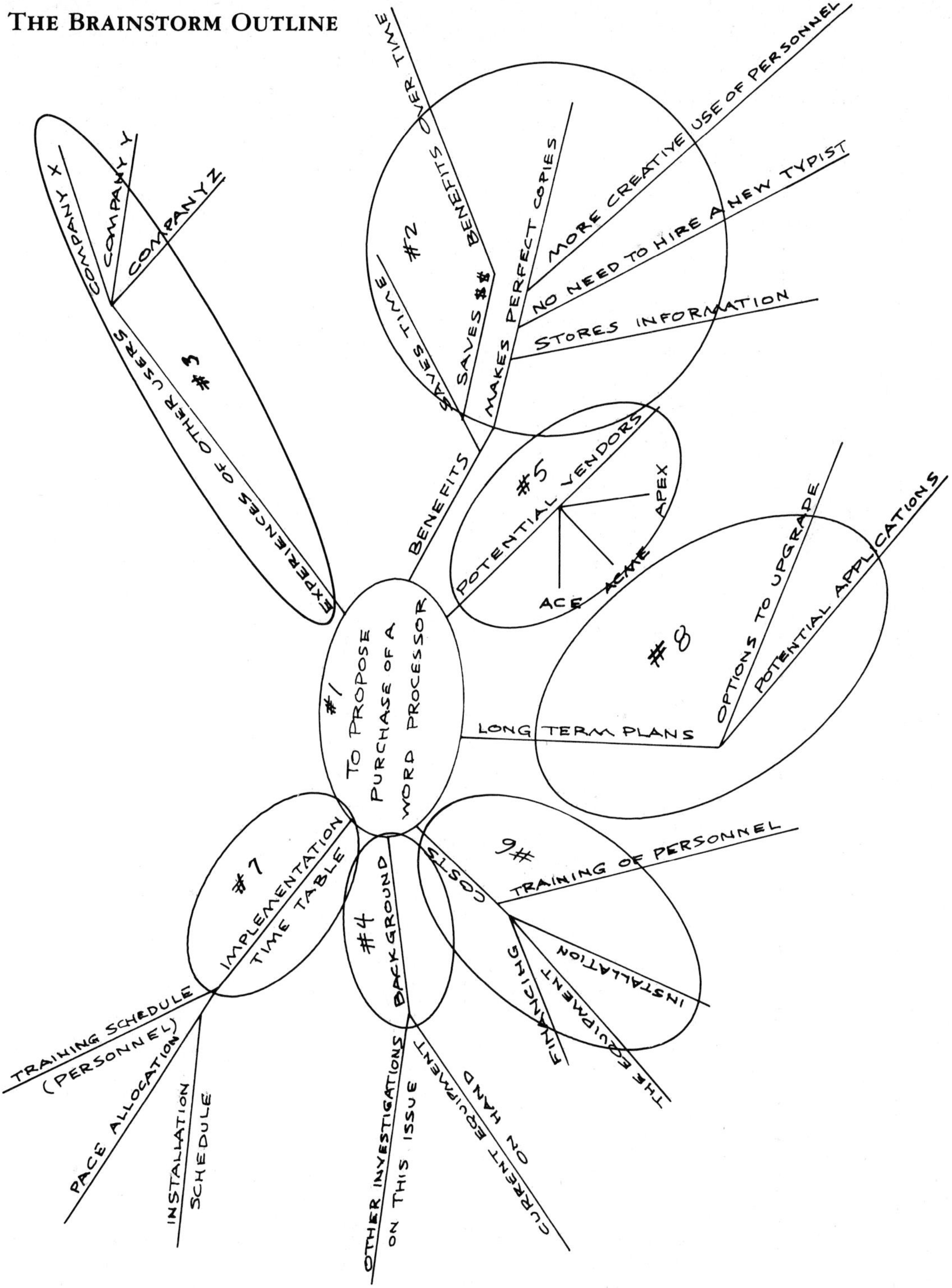
#1
TO PROPOSE PURCHASE OF A WORD PROCESSOR
BENEFITS
#2
BENEFITS OVER TIME
SAVES TIME
SAVES $$
MAKES PERFECT COPIES
MORE CREATIVE USE OF PERSONNEL
NO NEED TO HIRE A NEW TYPIST
STORES INFORMATION
#3
EXPERIENCES OF OTHER USERS
COMPANY X
COMPANY Y
COMPANY Z
#5
POTENTIAL VENDORS
APEX
ACME
ACE
#8
LONG TERM PLANS
OPTIONS TO UPGRADE
POTENTIAL APPLICATIONS
#6
COSTS
TRAINING OF PERSONNEL
INSTALLATION
THE EQUIPMENT
FINANCING
#4
BACKGROUND
OTHER INVESTIGATIONS ON THIS ISSUE
CURRENT EQUIPMENT ON HAND
#7
IMPLEMENTATION TIME TABLE
TRAINING SCHEDULE (PERSONNEL)
SPACE ALLOCATION
INSTALLATION SCHEDULE

FOR LONG REPORTS: Planning with Index Cards

Didn't you groan when you saw the teacher's pet smugly snap a rubber band around his term-paper index cards—at the same time you secretly wished you had followed his example?

When your report is long or requires extensive research, avoid a huge, unmanageable pileup of ideas and facts by using index cards. This time-tested strategy allows you to accumulate a large amount of material before deciding on a structure for presenting your message. You can shuffle the order of your ideas, discard irrelevant ones and add afterthoughts without wasting valuable time and energy rewriting. Later you will arrange your information into a framework that will form the skeleton of your report. Right now you need only concern yourself with gathering the "bones" that will comprise it.

How to do it

STEP 1: Take all notes on cards, including free-written ideas and insights. (See discussion of free writing, below.) Used this way, the cards function as a Brainstorm Outline. If you can express your idea in one sentence, don't feel you should add more information to the card. By limiting yourself to one idea per card, it will be easier to put the cards into the desired order later without rewriting. For lists of facts or statistics that take up more than one card, create your own system to key sections that belong together. A large color-coded dot in the upper right-hand corner works well.

STEP 2: Spread the cards out on your desk. Read through them and sort into piles according to similar topics. When you've finished, top off each pile with a "header card" so that you know the general contents of the piles by quickly glancing at the header. Put a rubber band around each pile.

STEP 3: Referring to your header cards, choose your Method of Development (see chapter 4) and arrange your banded piles accordingly.

STEP 4: Look back through each pile to be sure you like the order of ideas contained under each header card.

You've quickly created a skeleton that will support the body of your project. By using this time-saving method for getting started, you can afford to spend more time working on paragraphs.

ON YOUR OWN: Try preparing your next long report this way.

FOR LONG MEMOS & REPORTS: Post-It Note Tape

3M Post-It Note Tape, marketed for the first time in 1980, is a new product all writers should know about. Like the Brainstorm Outline and the index cards, Post-It Note Tape is a flexible method for developing an outline. The paperlike tape, packaged like a roll of cellophane tape, adheres to paper and vinyls. It's designed to be written or typed on and is available at most stationery stores. Because the pieces of Post-It Note Tape can be peeled up and moved about many times, you can rearrange them as often as necessary—no need to rewrite a word. No messy crossing out, no confusing arrows, no tiny scribbles in the margins—Post-It Note Tape can save you time.

How to plan a memo with the tape
    STEP 1: Cover a piece of paper with strips of tape four to five inches long. Use each strip as you would an index card—write down notes, phrases and ideas that you want to include in your memo. Fill as many strips as you need to cover all your main points. Don't hesitate to put down any idea —no matter how unimportant. You can always weed it out later.
    STEP 2: When you've finished note-making, experiment with different Methods of Development by changing the order of the strips. (See chapter 4, "Positioning Your Ideas: Choosing a Method of Development.") The tape peels up and resticks as many times as you like, so don't hesitate to rearrange the strips until the most appropriate sequence emerges. Explore all possibilities.
    STEP 3: As with index cards, you may want to color-code strips of tape for easy grouping. Related ideas should have the same colored dot or stripe on the left-hand edge of the strip. Offset subordinate ideas by indenting the strips of tape on the paper to make it resemble a traditional outline.

Now you're ready to start writing: one paragraph for each idea-bearing strip. Some executives I've worked with are so enthusiastic about the tape that they use it for all note-taking occasions. By doing this faithfully, they always have instant outlines, ready to expand into full reports.

How to use Post-It Note Tape for editing. This versatile tape can also be helpful when it's time to edit your memo or report. Use the tape to insert additional ideas or to make changes in the original ones. If you want to make a minor change, place the tape in the margin. Or, if you choose to make a more substantial change, simply cover the section with the tape and start over again.

You also can use the tape to make editorial comments to others. If you don't want to mark directly on the original copy of someone else's report, try placing the Post-It Note Tape in the margin and writing on it. Your comments will be received as a useful aside that can be easily removed.

Changing your mind about editorial comments, addressed to either yourself or others, is problem-free with the tape. Since you wrote on Post-It Note Tape, instead of on the paper, if you decide against a correction or comment, you can toss the tape away—not your report.

ON YOUR OWN: Using Post-it Note Tape, write a memo dealing with this situation:

> You recently interviewed a candidate for a job opening in your department. Write a memo evaluating the candidate's strengths and weaknesses. Do you recommend that the candidate be hired?

FOR ALL TYPES OF WRITING:
Liberate Your Thoughts with Free Writing

When to use. From time to time all of us feel too unhappy, confused or unsure of our own ideas to make a plan or list of any kind. Perhaps we're so intimidated by what others will think of our writing that we're blocked. If this happens to you, there is a special technique to help you set your ideas on paper. This approach is called free writing and it's used by many professional writers to limber up.

How to do it. Free writing means putting down on paper *everything* that comes to mind. As in free associating, the goal is to write down any and all ideas whether or not they are related to your topic. Try not to stop—don't answer the phone, don't stop for a cup of tea, just keep writing—even if you find yourself swearing on paper or writing about things that are off the topic. Don't worry about punctuation or word choice. If you can't immediately find the word you need, leave a blank and go on. Forget about complete sentences for now—use fragments, phrases, whatever emerges. Just don't stop producing words.

How free writing helps. Free writing can also be termed *pre*writing. It's like thinking on paper. Letting your thoughts range widely on any issues that come to mind—even personal ones—opens the channels for what you are really trying to say. This process helps you transfer those vague ideas circulating in your mind onto paper before they slip away. Once they are in black and white for you to read, others will soon follow.

Free writing helps you get rid of distracting thoughts that may be interfering with the serious writing you are trying to produce. When your mind keeps returning to last night's yoga class or the fifty dollars Cousin Nelson owes you, it's better to let all those distractions spill onto the paper, too. Soon the bothersome thoughts will be released, and your mind will feel clearer, ready for other tasks. If you remember an errand you must do later, such as picking up a loaf of bread on the way home, jot it down on a separate list. This, too, will liberate your mind.

Free writing is, in a way, like meditating. It removes the pressure to create a perfect product: anything you write down is acceptable. The mere act of writing in a nonstop, unfettered way will give you the confidence that more and more thoughts will emerge. Suddenly you have developed a rhythm. The pen is moving as if propelled across the page. This rhythm will stay with you—it gets you rolling the way warm-up exercises help you to jog or dance better.

Your plan seems to write itself. Free writing almost effortlessly generates tangible material for you to work with. After allowing all your relevant and irrelevant thoughts to quickly emerge, you will find a good number of salvageable ideas among them. Take a red pen and circle passages or sentences that represent a useful idea. You may be grateful and surprised to see that three pages of free writing has yielded enough information to create the framework for your outline.

Ideas emerging from free-writing exercises can be transferred to other Start-Up Strategies for further planning. Put words or phrases on a Brainstorm Outline, Post-It Note Tape, index cards or a regular outline.

The outpouring on page 32 from a confused and harried Hope Striver helped her to pull her thoughts together and to find a place to start.

Looking back at her scribbling, Hope found some useful ideas in it. She circled every word or phrase that seemed salvageable and tried to group similar ideas by numbering them (see page 33).

Hope used the free-writing exercise two more times, by which point she had generated enough ideas to make a good list of topics for her report. She also used the technique to develop some in-depth initial thinking on several of the ideas that emerged in her first free-writing effort. In the end she had created a clear outline, ready to develop into a first draft.

ON YOUR OWN: To practice free writing, fill as many sheets of paper as you can with your perceptions as you sit writing. What do you hear, see, touch, feel? Write as quickly as you can without concern for sentence structure or organization. Don't revise.

Note: This exercise is more than a good Start-Up technique. It is also designed to relieve you of the bad habit of thinking too much about mechanics during the first draft. More on this later.

HOPE'S FREE-WRITING WARM-UP

I can't believe it. Here I am chained again to my desk with
this stupid report to write and old baldy breathing down my
neck to finish it. Why me? I'd much rather be at the sales
conference shaking hands and hearing that keynote speaker
—what was his name?—who's done so much research on
building robots—the wave of the future—I can't wait to
have my *own*.

Anyway . . . I'm getting warmed up here . . . maybe writing
isn't so bad . . . using these dots between my words helps
. . . I don't even have to think about punctuation . . .
Anyway what's my topic? Oh yes . . . an analysis of text
processing usage by different departments to see 1) if
it's being used fairly, 2) to try to figure out if any one
department is hogging it all, 3) to see if we may need to
enhance the system soon because our needs seem to be
growing so quickly, 4) is this really true or are people
just squawking because they want instant access and
service? Hmm that's a tall order. Where shall I start?
Also, what about coming up with a fair amount of time that
users should expect to wait for their processing? How to
determine this?? Well I guess I could include the
interviews I've collected from everyone plus the
statistics on machine usage that Jamie gathered. What
else? Maybe do my own survey of projected needs? I should
be sure to ask about 1) projected staff increases, 2) new
projects anticipated, 3) staff turnover requiring
reorientation toward equipment and usage procedures. Oh
it's so hard to concentrate on this. I wonder if it's
raining out. Did I take that steak out of the freezer for
tonight?—oooh I'd better call Betty and see. But no, I
must not allow distractions. I promised myself I'd keep
writing for twenty minutes no matter what happened. Let's
see what else can I put into my report?

HOPE'S FREE-WRITING WARM-UP, WITH IDEAS CIRCLED

I can't believe it. Here I am chained again to my desk with
this stupid report to write and old baldy breathing down my
neck to finish it. Why me? I'd much rather be at the sales
conference shaking hands and hearing that keynote speaker
—what was his name?—who's done so much research on
building robots—the wave of the future—I can't wait to
have my *own*.

Anyway . . . I'm getting warmed up here . . . maybe writing
isn't so bad . . . using these dots between my words helps
. . . I don't even have to think about punctuation . . .
Anyway what's my topic? Oh yes . . . an analysis of text
processing usage by different departments to see 1) if
it's being used fairly, 2) to try to figure out if any one
department is hogging it all, 3) to see if we may need to
enhance the system soon because our needs seem to be
growing so quickly, 4) is this really true or are people
just squawking because they want instant access and
service? Hmm that's a tall order. Where shall I start?
Also, what about coming up with a fair amount of time that
users should expect to wait for their processing? How to
determine this?? Well I guess I could include the
interviews I've collected from everyone plus the
statistics on machine usage that Jamie gathered. What
else? Maybe do my own survey of projected needs? I should
be sure to ask about 1) projected staff increases, 2) new
projects anticipated, 3) staff turnover requiring
reorientation toward equipment and usage procedures. Oh
it's so hard to concentrate on this. I wonder if it's
raining out. Did I take that steak out of the freezer for
tonight?—oooh I'd better call Betty and see. But no, I
must not allow distractions. I promised myself I'd keep
writing for twenty minutes no matter what happened. Let's
see what else can I put into my report?

3
The
Right Look

Before moving on to the topics of putting your ideas in order and writing the first draft, let's stop to discuss an all-important factor in business writing success: how any memo or report should look when you're finished writing it. (You already know how a letter should look.) If you have an image of how your writing will appear on the page, you can work toward this visual goal even as you begin to write.

So far, I have given you strategies for developing a list of ideas or topics to guide your writing. You will eventually elaborate each separate idea in a separate paragraph. This chapter explains the importance of paragraph headlines for visual impact, organizing, persuading your reader and keeping you, the writer, on target.

Headlines. As you can see in this book, I label almost every subsection with an italicized headline. The headlines are the basic ideas in each paragraph. Once you know your headlines or ideas, it's easy to write a paragraph on each one. Whether you arrive at your headlines from the Start-Up Sheet, Brainstorm Outline or free writing, the fact is that once you have them, the hardest part of writing—the conceptual part—is finished.

The right look. Every page you write must be visually appealing. Clear writing alone is not enough. The essence of your memo, letter or report must jump off the page, enticing the reader with its format.

Consciously and unconsciously, readers develop an attitude toward your writing from its appearance even before they begin to read it. You must take advantage of every opportunity to reach out to your readers. Let your format work *for* you —not against you.

Below and on the following pages you will find two memos. Don't read them; just look at them. Which do you like better at first glance?

TO: All editorial and production unit chiefs

FROM: Ed Dittor, Managing Editor, *The Daily Muse*

RE: Meeting June 30 to discuss conversion to video
       display equipment in newsroom

DATE: June 23, 1984

The Zap Video Company has made an intriguing presentation to the publisher that we "go automated" and update the newsroom with video display equipment. The publisher has asked me to discuss the proposal with other top staff for their opinions.

There will be a meeting in my office on June 30, 1984, at 10:00 A.M. If you cannot attend, let me know within two days whom you will be sending in your place.

Zap feels that we will be able to buck the trend of declining revenue if we convert to its video display system. They say that our productivity will increase dramatically, our paper will run with fewer typographical mistakes, and it's a proven morale booster for writers, editors and the production staff.

Zap is aware of our weak financial situation. They, on the other hand, are in a good cash position at the moment and are willing to offer us excellent financing terms if we can quickly decide to go with their system. The company has given us two months to act.

There are several advantages in converting to video. To start with, writers will be able to get their copy out more quickly, once they become familiar with the system. Copy editors will also be able to do their job faster from the cleanly displayed version of stories that they will see. Edited stories can be sent to the production room instantly by pushing a button, thus reducing the time writers and editors will spend going up and down the stairs to the production room.

(continued)

Gradually, we will be able to put our library on the system and code stories by writer, headline, first paragraph or whole story. This is likely to mean that our writers will get more research done with much greater speed. (For description of other advantages, see the enclosed Zap Video promotional material.)

We do expect some problems, however, in converting to video. There will be significant union opposition to conversion. There's no other way to look at it: this means a loss of jobs, especially on the production side. Another factor we must also consider is financing. We will run up added costs in other areas, for example: new work desks must be purchased and the whole building will have to be rewired. I will distribute a complete cost projection memo before the meeting for your consideration. Finally, every operation will be in for a serious interruption while people are trained in the use of the new equipment.

TO: All editorial and production unit chiefs

FROM: Ed Dittor, Managing Editor, *The Daily Muse*

DATE: June 23, 1984

RE: Meeting June 30 to discuss conversion to video display equipment in newsroom

Purpose of meeting
The Zap Video Company has made an intriguing presentation to the publisher that we "go automated" and update the newsroom with video display equipment. The publisher has asked me to discuss the proposal with other top staff for their opinions.

Meeting information
Where: My office
When: June 30, 1984, 10:00 A.M.
Note: If you cannot attend, let me know within two days whom you will be sending in your place.

Zap Video's recommendation
Zap feels that we will be able to buck the trend of declining revenue if we convert to its video display system. They say that our productivity will increase dramatically, our paper will run with fewer typographical mistakes, and it's a proven morale booster for writers, editors and the production staff.

Importance of a quick decision
Zap is aware of our weak financial situation. They, on the other hand, are in a good cash position at the moment, and are willing to offer us excellent financial terms if we can quickly decide to go with their system. The company has given us two months to act.

Advantages of converting to video
- Once they become familiar with the system, writers will be able to get their copy out more quickly.
- Copy editors will be able to do their job faster from the cleanly displayed version of stories that they will see on the screen.
- Edited stories can be sent to the production room instantly by pushing a button, thus reducing the time writers and editors will spend going up and down the stairs to the production room.
- Gradually we can put our library on the system and can code stories by writer, headline, first paragraph or whole story. This is likely to mean that our writers will get more research done with much greater speed.
- See description of other advantages on the enclosed Zap Video promotional material.

Problems converting to video
- There will be significant union opposition to conversion. There's no other way to look at it: this means a loss of jobs, especially on the production side.
- We will run up added costs in other areas: new work desks must be purchased and the whole building will have to be rewired. I will distribute a complete cost projection memo before the meeting for your consideration.
- Every operation will be in for a serious interruption while people are trained in the use of the new equipment.

Why did you prefer the second memo? If you chose the second one, no doubt it was because the crisp, clean effect created by the headlines and ample white space appealed to your eye. Headlining means choosing a few words that illustrate the content of the paragraph and leading with them; headlines have a dramatic visual impact.

Headlines help the reader get the message. Business writing is different from other types of writing: its primary goal is to get straight to the point—to get a message across.

Headlines make ideas leap off the page at the reader. Thanks to headlines, readers who are in a hurry can skim through the memo or report and zero in on the section that interests them. *You* may have toiled over every sentence, but your readers may not want to read every paragraph you've written.

Headlines keep you on target. Use headlines to make sure that each paragraph focuses on only one idea. If you find you come up with two very different headlines for one paragraph, you have not developed one clear and concise idea. Write two different paragraphs instead. You will learn more about paragraphs in chapter 5, called "Writing the First Draft."

Headlines make information easier to find. Readers are generally looking for something specific. It is your job to help them find it. By using headlines, you make it easier for your readers to find the section that applies to them or to relocate on second reading a section they found particularly important. Think how grateful you would be to find in the files a well-headlined report on a subject you're researching. You could sift through it instantly to see if the ideas were helpful.

Headlines make information more accessible and more understandable. And readers appreciate it when the information they are looking for is easy to find, just as if they were reading the morning newspaper.

Are headlines necessary for every memo and report? Most emphatically, yes! Today's readers are so busy and distracted that they don't have time to read carefully. Headlining is the natural solution to the overwhelming amounts of reading that all managers face—what Alvin Toffler called information overload. Every day, in-baskets fill with piles of memos, reports, contracts, proposals, fliers, minutes from meetings and more. There just isn't enough time in the day to sit down and carefully read every item. Since most reading is done in a hurry, it is up to the writer to help the reader as much as possible by labeling all ideas. If your memo looks easy to read, it is more likely to be read.

What about letters? Unfortunately, headlines are not yet acceptable on letters. They seem to violate the personal quality of the letter. Nevertheless, for your own

Issues We All Face

planning purposes, it will be helpful for you to use headlines in writing the first draft of a letter—you can always remove them later.

Use "RE:" on your letters. Here's an idea that will greatly improve your letters. Write a reference headline at the top of each letter, just beneath the inside address. By starting with the helpful "RE: Topic of this letter," you are doing the reader an important favor. Make your writing cry out to be read by adding this teaser at the start. Here's an example.

```
                                                   June 2, 1980


Mr. Edwin Newman
National Broadcasting Company, Inc.
Thirty Rockefeller Plaza
New York, NY 10020


RE: How to locate your movie, "Strictly Speaking"


Dear Mr. Newman:

I run a consulting firm in Boston for improving executive
communications skills. I'd like to expand my seminars by
showing your movie, "Strictly Speaking"; it would be a
helpful addition. However, I've been unable to find a copy
of it in the Boston area.

Please send me information on buying or renting your film.
I'd greatly appreciate it.


Cordially,


Deborah Dumaine
President


DD:RK
```

Headlines meet the same need that computers were invented to meet: the need to organize large amounts of information meaningfully. Computers use labels and categories to help the user "key into" the data they offer. Because all categories are carefully labeled and stored, one can call up information for review at a moment's notice. Headlines serve the same function—they allow the reader easy access to the information in a report or memo. Out of sheer necessity, headlining is rapidly becoming the writing approach for this decade.

The following exercise gives you a chance to start using headlines. Try it now.

Choosing Your Headlines
Directions: Write an appropriate headline in each blank space. Don't peek at the answers!

```
TO:    Director, Property Management
FROM:  Vice-President, Human Resources
RE:    Possible correlation between employee health and
       physical environment in the Jarvis Wing
```

_____

A recent statistical study of absenteeism revealed a 23% increase in midday illness and afternoon sick leave during the past 10 months. The increase occurs exclusively in the four departments that moved from the main building to the newly constructed Jarvis Wing 10 months ago.

_____

The Personnel Division requests that the Planning Division undertake an immediate study of the Jarvis Wing. This situation is urgent. We suggest that the study include investigation of noise level, lighting level, light fixtures and other outlets. The study should search for potentially toxic substances in or emissions from insulation, wall, floor and ceiling materials and air-circulation systems in the Jarvis Wing.

_____

1. This company is legally responsible for providing a safe work environment for its employees.
2. The operation and productivity of this company depend on the efficient functioning of the departments located in the Jarvis Wing.

The departments concerned are Accounting, Central
Records, Research, Word Processing. These departments
moved to the new quarters because they all needed
extensive installation of automated systems. As required,
these departments instituted comprehensive training and
reorientation programs. Nevertheless, heads of the
departments report decreases from levels of efficiency
and accuracy previous to the move, as well as the
above-mentioned increases in afternoon sick leave.

In response to the statistical study of absenteeism, this
department circulated a health questionnaire among
employees of the four departments located in the Jarvis
Wing. The questionnaire revealed the following specific
physical complaints:
1. Headache or migraine   3. General fatigue
2. Unusual eye fatigue   4. Impaired ability to
                                      concentrate

The complaints identified by the health questionnaire
strongly suggest that something is wrong in the work
environment, and that further study of the problem is
absolutely necessary.

Now compare your answers with the ones on pages 42–43. Don't worry if they are not exactly alike. If your headlines seem to match in meaning, you're on the right track!

The most commonly used headlines. The number of possible headlines for any report or memo is enormous. But once you know what type of report you are working on, you will be able to eliminate many inappropriate headlines. Somehow, we seem to use certain headlines again and again. Here are the kinds of headlines I see most commonly used at company after company.

Statement of a Problem	Explanation of Cause or	Results of a Study
Statement of Purpose	Effect	Considerations
Background Information	Directions	How to
Supporting Data	Explanation of a Process	Scope

Implications	Evaluation	Summary
Description	Proposal	Conclusion
What Happened	Suggestions	Action Requested
What Was Observed	Recommendations	Implementation Plan
Analysis	Request	Action to Be Taken

Choosing the best headlines for your memos and reports. This is a partial list of the most common types of writing that I see in my workshops. How many of your memos or reports fall into these categories?

Annual Report	Performance Appraisal	Request for Proposal
Announcement of a	Pinpointing a Problem	(RFP)
Meeting	Planning Report	Research Results
Audit Report	Problem-Solving Memo	Sales Report
Decision-Needed Memo	Procedural Change	Status Report
Engineering Report	Notice	Training Materials
Feasibility Study	Procedural Manual	Trip Report
Informative Memo	Proposal	Work Order
Minutes of a Meeting	Recommendation Report	
Organizational Memo	Request for Information	

Now let's match some typical headlines with some typical reports. I want to offer you models—complete with headlines—for structuring a few sample reports, even though I know this is a bit dangerous because it might encourage you to be lazy.

Every report is different and should be given your most creative effort. The sample headlines I offer should inspire you by giving you a jumping-off point. If

---

TO: Director, Property Management

FROM: Vice-President, Human Resources

RE: Possible correlation between employee health and physical environment in the Jarvis Wing

Problem
A recent statistical study of absenteeism revealed a 23% increase in midday illness and afternoon sick leave during the past 10 months. The increase occurs exclusively in the four departments that moved from the main building to the newly constructed Jarvis Wing 10 months ago.

Action Requested

The Personnel Division requests that the Planning Division undertake an immediate study of the Jarvis Wing. This situation is urgent. We suggest that the study include investigation of noise level, lighting level, light fixtures and other outlets. The study should search for potentially toxic substances in or emissions from insulation, wall, floor and ceiling materials and air-circulation systems in the Jarvis Wing.

Rationale

1. This company is legally responsible for providing a safe work environment for its employees.
2. The operation and productivity of this company depend on the efficient functioning of the departments located in the Jarvis Wing.

Background

The departments concerned are Accounting, Central Records, Research, Word Processing. These departments moved to the new quarters because they all needed extensive installation of automated systems. As required, these departments instituted comprehensive training and reorientation programs. Nevertheless, heads of the departments report decreases from levels of efficiency and accuracy previous to the move, as well as the above-mentioned increases in afternoon sick leave.

Specific Complaints

In response to the statistical study of absenteeism, this department circulated a health questionnaire among employees of the four departments located in the Jarvis Wing. The questionnaire revealed the following specific physical complaints:

1. Headache or migraine
2. Unusual eye fatigue
3. General fatigue
4. Impaired ability to concentrate

Summary

The complaints identified by the health questionnaire strongly suggest that something is wrong in the work environment, and that further study of the problem is absolutely necessary.

you simply adopt them without considering the special needs of your project, you could end up with a disastrous piece of writing. Therefore, the following lists are suggestions only. Never let them take the place of your own seriously analyzed ideas.

Typical Headlines for Common Memos & Reports

MEETING ANNOUNCEMENT
1. Time and place of meeting
2. Agenda: a list of topics
3. Speakers
4. Background
   - events leading to calling of meeting
   - what you hope to accomplish
5. Information to consider
6. How to prepare for the meeting
7. Contact/person in charge

DECISION-NEEDED MEMO
1. Overview
2. Issue
3. Recommended action
   - who is involved in the "action"
   - schedule of steps to be taken
   - pros and cons
   - subsequent meetings
4. Background
   - why it became an issue
5. Other decisions/options
   - pros & cons for each
6. Results of study
7. Summary

STATUS REPORT
1. Overview
2. Subject
3. Current status: progress to date
4. Successful aspects
5. Problems encountered
6. Planned solutions
   - further information needed
   - opinion needed
   - decision needed
   - request for confirmation of plan
7. Other projects completed
   - summary of each
8. Other projects still in progress
   - background
   - status
   - forecast of (a) time schedule, (b) changes, (c) cost
9. Summary

PERFORMANCE ANALYSIS
1. Overview (of results)
2. Process or task analyzed
3. Problems detected
   - description of problems
   - possible causes of problems
4. Suggested solutions
   - people involved
   - cost (if any) involved
   - time involved
5. Comparison with previous model
   - similarities
   - differences
6. Dates for changes to be made
7. Date of next evaluation
8. Summary

SOLVING A PROBLEM
1. Overview
2. Problem
3. Recommended solution
4. Persuaders
5. Background
   - symptoms
   - causes

REQUEST TO PURCHASE
1. Overview
2. Recommendation (state what you want)
   - predicted productivity improvements
   - economic advantages
3. Analysis of items in question
   - cost justification

REQUEST FOR PROPOSAL
1. Overview
2. Service/item required
3. Background
   - relevant information
4. Possible problems

PROPOSAL
1. Overview
2. The proposal stated
3. Supporting reasons
4. Plan
   - scope
   - schedule
   - budget
   - implementation

- previous problems/solutions in comparison
6. Alternative solutions
   - pros & cons
7. Summary
   - problem restated
   - action requested (restated)

- depreciation
- brand selection
4. Implementation considerations
   - timetable
   - plan
5. Staffing requirements
6. Background
7. Summary

5. Budget considerations
6. Outline of response needed
7. Deadline for submission
8. Contact person
9. Summary

5. Points to investigate further
   - other people involved
   - time factors
6. Conclusions
   - restate recommendation/proposal
7. Summary

REMEMBER: Headlines clarify the issues quickly and dramatically, giving your message the extra edge it needs to stand out from the other papers on an executive's desk. Keep the goal of a visually strong presentation in mind whenever you start to write!

4
Positioning Your Ideas
Choosing a Method of Development

METHODS OF DEVELOPMENT FOR ORGANIZING LETTERS, MEMOS AND REPORTS

There are many ways to organize your ideas; these organizing principles are referred to as Methods of Development (M.O.D.'s). An M.O.D. is a way to structure your ideas within a sentence, paragraph, letter or memo, or within an entire report. It describes how ideas relate to each other or in what order they appear. Choose an M.O.D. according to the needs of your reader, your goal for the subject matter, and the way your ideas naturally hang together. Some of these M.O.D.'s may overlap a bit, or you may find yourself using them in combination. This is perfectly acceptable.

Here are the most common Methods of Development:

1. Order of importance
   a. Most important to least important
   b. Least important to most important
2. Chronology
3. Sequence
4. Organization in space
5. Comparison
6. Specific to General *or* General to Specific
7. Analysis

Why is it essential to organize your message? If your reader is the harried executive who only reads the first paragraph, the answer is obvious. But there are other reasons, too.

Clear writing is a sign of clear thinking. If you can't put your thoughts together logically, you probably don't really know what you're talking about. Your mental disorganization will be quite obvious when it's splayed across a sheet of paper. And your reader will judge you by it. As David Belasco, the great American theatrical producer said, "If you can't write your idea on the back of my calling card, you don't have a clear idea."

Being able to organize your ideas means being able to separate what's most important from what's least important. It also means labeling your ideas so that you can see what categories they fall into. Is your sentence a solution? a cause? a symptom? a summary? an example? This is why headlines are so important.

Now that you're using headlines (you *are* using headlines, right?), it will be easy for you to review your ideas in order to select the right M.O.D. A label on every paragraph is a great help in choosing the sequence for your topics.

Let's take a close look at each method.

METHOD OF DEVELOPMENT #1: Order of Importance

A. Most important to least important
I begin with this method because it is the best solution to so many writing projects. It is particularly useful in memos or reports that must report findings or offer important recommendations.

The exercise below lists the segments that might appear in a typical two-page memo. Try arranging the mixed-up segments in order of importance from most to least by numbering them. Keep in mind that your goal is to persuade a reader (who you feel is open to your suggestions) to adopt your ingenious new recommendation for improving efficiency in the mail-order department.

MEMO A

1._____Problem description   4._____Background
2._____Problem analysis and   5._____Your recommendation
        supporting data   6._____Final summary
3._____Implementation plan

How did you do? In making your choices you should have asked yourself, "What is the most important information I must convey?" This information should appear as close to the beginning of the report as possible. The best order for the segments is:

MEMO A

1. Problem description   4. Problem analysis and supporting data
2. Your recommendation   5. Implementation plan
3. Background   6. Final summary

REMEMBER: Whenever possible, state your "bottom line" at the top.

Now let's try another example. Here we have a long in-depth report proposing your idea for solving the same problem in the mail-order department. The components are rather different. Again, arrange them from most important to least important.

REPORT B: Proposal for Improving Efficiency in the Mail-Order Department
1._____Advantages and disadvantages of your recommendation
2._____Your recommendation and supporting reasons
3._____Statement of problem and analysis
4._____Conclusion
5._____Overview (abstract)
6._____Implementation plan

How did you do? First take a minute to compare your answers with mine, below. What makes Report B different from Memo A? It's the inclusion of the "Overview" at the beginning—an essential addition to writing over two pages long. The overview summarizes the problem and its solution very briefly so that the reader is immediately oriented to the contents of the report. Then you begin the report proper. In fact, the ideas in the two documents are arranged very similarly, despite the fact that the sections have different headlines. If your background information is not terribly important or if your supporting data are excessively long, you should consider including these items much later in the report, possibly after the implementation plan. In the conclusion, summarize briefly your recommendation and best reasons once more.

MEMO A: Suggested Order	REPORT B: Suggested Order
1. Problem description	1. Overview
2. Your recommendation	2. Statement of problem and analysis
3. Background	3. Your recommendation and supporting reasons
4. Problem analysis and supporting data	4. Advantages and disadvantages of your recommendation
5. Implementation plan	5. Implementation plan
6. Final summary	6. Conclusion

What do the two outlines have in common? In each case they begin by stating the most important ideas first. In business writing, the key information should almost always be right at the beginning where the manager can quickly learn what he or she really wants to know. Whether you label this information "overview" or any other word is immaterial. This "bottom line" information can appear in many guises. Here are a few typical headlines.

Conclusions	Action Requested	Proposal summarized
Recommendations	Results	
Abstract	Overview	

The order of your ideas is important even in a single paragraph. What single change could you make that would greatly improve the effectiveness of the following short memo?

```
RE: A Coordination Clerk

The need for photocopying services is one of the fastest
growing in the company. Copying requests from all
departments are submitted to the Purchasing Division
because the copy machine is located here. However, we are
the only division without a control clerk assigned. As a
result, the copy-related accounting, reorder of paper and
repair calls are not coordinated. Because of the overall
volume of work being handled by the Purchasing Division,
and the steadily increasing demand for the service, these
functions can no longer be performed by a department of
this size. It is essential that we add a coordination clerk
to the Purchasing Division.
```

How did you do? Ed Itwell put the last sentence in this memo first. And he was right. The big problem with the memo is that the most important sentence is at the very end. When he first read it, Ed thought the memo was a history of the growth of photocopying services in the company.

Also, the headline, "RE: A Coordination Clerk," is not helpful enough. The memo would have more impact if it said, "RE: The Need to Hire a Coordination Clerk."

REMEMBER: Whenever possible, put your most important information at the beginning of your writing, either in summary or in complete form.

USEFUL FOR: Research reports, proposals, announcements, evaluations, status reports, forecasts, procedural change notices, sales reports.

B. Least Important to Most Important

An exception: the shocking proposal. Sometimes your suggestion, request or conclusion is just too controversial to use as an opener. Understanding your readers is always the key to successful writing, and some readers can't handle a forthright, up-front request. Perhaps your memo proposes an unexpected solution to a problem, or a request for something already denied. If you fear your readers will stop at the bad news, you will have to be more subtle, by putting your persuasive ideas first. The "persuaders" will help to lead the readers through your ideas until you bring them around to your point of view.

Remember when Rick Cotta had to introduce the upsetting idea of a time clock to his employees? What if he'd written it as on page 51, with the bad news first?

Let's look again at the memo as it first appeared in chapter 1, arranged from least important to most important (page 52).

Which memo did you prefer? Which would be most easily accepted? Which shows an understanding of people's psychological needs? In the second memo, the appealing and persuasive information is at the beginning, where it will be most effective. The second memo is clearly better.

Whether you present information from least to most important or most to least important can have major consequences. If a series of reasons will help the readers understand your position, it is best to build from proof to proposition. You are leading your readers to your conclusion.

In the following situation the question appeared in a slightly different form: should Hope present her opinion first and reasons later? or vice versa? Here's what happened.

For a long time, Hope and all the other top managers had felt that Rob Ott deserved a promotion and raise. His sales figures were the highest at Polytrix, and he had even started a sales training program to share his successful strategies.

Ed had recently hinted to Hope that Rob was feeling discontent at Polytrix, but no one believed he would actually leave. Then Hope found a copy of Rob's updated résumé in the Xerox machine and realized Ed knew more than he was telling. It was time to write a letter to the president to grant Rob the long-overdue promotion immediately. In her memo, Hope chose to present her reasons first and her opinion last. Why? Because she knew that the president, who was on the austerity warpath, would not read beyond the words "salary increase." First, she had to alert him to Rob's possible resignation and remind him of his value to the company. Rob was too important an asset to lose.

In this way, Hope enticed the president into reading the entire contents of her startling memo. Had the economic state of the company been better and had the president been in a spending mood, Hope could have opened with her opinion and, with luck, secured Rob's promotion.

MEMORANDUM

TO: All manufacturing unit personnel

FROM: Rick Cotta

DATE: April 21, 1984

RE: Installation of time clock and other benefits

Announcement
As of May 1, 1984, a time clock will be installed in the
manufacturing unit. I am concerned that everyone is not
contributing an equal day's work for an equal day's pay.
Most of you are punctual and many put in more hours than are
expected. However, there are a few among you who do not
work a full day.

To recognize those who are on time and to prevent their
feeling cheated by those who are not putting in their share
of work, management feels it necessary to install the
clock.

Starting next month each person in the manufacturing unit
will punch in and out to record the actual number of hours
worked each week. Although this may seem to be a harsh
remedy to some of you, there is a hidden benefit: flextime
can now be established.

New Policy: FLEXTIME
Many of you have asked to start work earlier in the day and
leave earlier, or to work eight hours starting later in the
day. We realize that we can institute this new policy now
that we are installing a time clock. The clock will allow
you to create your own hours (see attached list of
acceptable work schedules). Please take note of the fact
that you can leave early on Friday if you've gotten ahead
of yourself for the week.

Meeting Planned
I will announce a meeting soon so that we can discuss how
the time clock system will work and any concerns you may
have.

TO: All yogurt manufacturing unit personnel

FROM: Rick Cotta

DATE: April 21, 1984

RE: New personnel policies: Flextime

Background

For some time now here at Creemytrix, both management and
manufacturing personnel have suggested that work time
should be more efficiently and flexibly scheduled.
Management has been concerned that it does not have an
adequate method of determining who works when. And
manufacturing personnel have complained that the current
work schedule does not take into account the personal
needs of workers.

These schedules worked for us four years ago, when we were
smaller, but with our recent growth it's time for a change.
Several meetings have been held over the past few months,
and the following plans have been adopted.

Flextime

Starting next month, each person in the manufacturing unit
will be able to determine his or her own work week schedule
within certain guidelines. (See attached list of
acceptable work hours.) If a worker wishes to start and
complete the workday earlier, that will now be possible.
Conversely, the workday may start and end later. Also, it
will be possible to "get a jump on the weekend" by leaving
earlier on Friday if the weekly work has been completed.

Keeping track of hours

To keep track of hours worked each week, a time clock will
be installed in the manufacturing unit. Punching in will
take some getting used to, but after the initial and
anticipated confusion, the system should run smoothly.

Meeting to be announced

In a few days, I will announce the date and time of a
meeting to cover how the time clock arrangement will work.
Please be prepared to discuss any and all concerns you may
have. As soon as we iron out the kinks, the flextime policy
can be put into effect. This new system should make the
work week proceed more smoothly for all of us.

Another way to present information persuasively is to state your opinion or theory first, then prove it with supporting evidence. If your conclusion clarifies the sentences that uphold it, state it first. Perhaps your opinion has more impact at the beginning than at the end.

To decide whether you should present opinion-reasons or reasons-opinion, ask yourself, "How will my readers react?" Choose the presentation that will convince your readers. Be careful not to lose your proposition in the middle.

METHOD OF DEVELOPMENT #2: Chronology

When you need to summarize the history of a product or situation stressing its relationship to time, use a chronological M.O.D. Accident reports and progress reports are typically arranged in time order. The data of each event or change will structure your plan. If you use this method, beware of getting too involved in detail. Stick to major, consequential facts. Your goal is to provide a quick, easy-to-follow review or plan.

There are two major problems with using this type of development. First, the time order may force important material to appear in an unemphatic position—such as the middle. Unimportant issues may get more emphasis by occupying the beginning and end. In this case, state the most important idea or recommendation at the beginning, ignoring time association. Then shift to chronological development. It saves the hurried reader time digging out pertinent information.

Second, chronological order can be monotonous. Don't begin each sentence with a date. Give your sentences variety by putting time words in different places. This is guaranteed to be more appealing to your reader.

USEFUL FOR: Processes, growth statistics, accident reports, trip results, test results, progress reports, manufacturing and scientific procedures, journals, minutes of meetings, planning reports.

METHOD OF DEVELOPMENT #3: Sequence

Sequence or step by step. Sequential organization means presenting your material step by step as if you were writing instructions or a recipe. Each step may be as important as the next. Sequence is different from chronology in that there is no mention of *when* the actions must take place, only that they must occur in a particular order. Make sure you really understand the task or process you are describing so that your points will appear in the correct place. A sequential M.O.D. is useful for explaining a chemical process or how to operate a piece of machinery.

USEFUL FOR: Instructions, descriptions of processes, handbooks, instruction manuals.

METHOD OF DEVELOPMENT #4:
Organization in Space

Organize your writing spatially when you're dealing with different locations. You may be reporting statistics geographically in a sales report that starts on the East Coast and moves across the country to the West Coast, or by your company's sales office locations. Spatial order doesn't have to be on a grand scale. You can use it to describe detail on your new office computer from left to right, top to bottom, or exterior to interior.

With this M.O.D., you can create a coherent and concrete order that's easy to follow. It's like connecting the dots in a child's dot-to-dot book. You're given the dots—can you connect them in a way that creates the neatest picture? (Unlike in a dot-to-dot book, there may be more than one good structure that works.)

As you lead your readers from place to place, you create a visual image for them —it's like giving them a map.

One warning: Spatial organization in long reports can be just as monotonous as the chronological method. Make a conscious effort to vary sentences and substitute new phrases for overused ones. Try not to be mechanical.

USEFUL FOR: Development reports, descriptions of machinery, building sites, inventions, sales research reports (by specific company division, district, East-West, United States–overseas).

METHOD OF DEVELOPMENT #5: Comparison

Comparison is juxtaposing things to emphasize similarities and differences or advantages and disadvantages. For example, you may be asked to study and evaluate two possible sites for your new downtown office. The best way to present this type of comparison is first to describe all the advantages of both sites. Then present the disadvantages of the two sites.

Avoid mixing statements about advantages and disadvantages in the same section. This confuses readers. Arrange your comparison this way:

1. Advantages—Site A and Site B
2. Disadvantages—Site A and Site B

instead of this way:

1. Site A—advantages and disadvantages
2. Site B—advantages and disadvantages

Be coherent in your comparisons by using key phrases, such as:

- on one hand
- the latter
- in the same way
- in opposition to this
- on the other
- in this way
- on the contrary
- although that is true
- the former
- in contrast
- but then

Comparisons are valuable for explaining the unfamiliar to your reader by relating it to the familiar. When comparing two subjects, always mention the more familiar one first. This is the best way to help the reader to understand the lesser-known subject. For example, if you were trying to explain an airplane to someone who'd never seen one, you'd start by comparing it to a bird. Alien ideas have often been understood by comparison: the Indians called the first trains "iron horses."

Beware of comparing too much technical information in writing, if graphs or charts would be more helpful.

USEFUL FOR: Feasibility studies, research results, planning reports, some proposals.

METHOD OF DEVELOPMENT #6:
Specific to General or General to Specific

This M.O.D. helps you inform, instruct or persuade your reader. If your challenge is to present a general idea and the specifics (or examples) that describe it, which should come first? This depends on whether or not your reader is already acquainted with the subject matter.

For example, what if you had to explain a camera to a cave man? He probably wouldn't show a jot of interest in the little black box unless you first presented the specifics: a neat snapshot of his bludgeon, a record of his greatest hunting feats, the excitement of instant development and—most remarkable—a picture of himself. You would be leading him to understanding from specifics to the general idea: camera.

On the other hand, what if you were explaining the latest high-tech camera to an expert photographer? Obviously, you'd start by mentioning the camera and then proceed to describe its fantastic features. The photographer is already familiar with the concept of a camera, so it makes sense to open with it. You're reminding him of something familiar to orient him to the subsequent new information about the camera's special options.

If you're deciding whether to present specifics or generality first and your goal is to persuade, reread Hope's reasons-opinion decision in M.O.D. #1; the principle is the same. Consider the specifics to be your reasons and the generality your opinion.

USEFUL FOR: Proposals, feasibility reports, work orders, training materials.

METHOD OF DEVELOPMENT #7: Analysis

Use an analytical M.O.D. to interpret the how and why of a situation by taking it apart. Your mechanic uses the same process when he disassembles your car's engine to find out what's wrong. This format is a logical one for analyzing data you've collected. Description of parts will lead to a clear overall assessment.

Imagine you're writing an evaluation for a venture capitalist, Mr. Terry Z., who is trying to decide whether to invest everything he has in the latest high-tech mousetrap. You've been given a twenty-page report documenting its research and development. How should you analyze the report to help Mr. Z. decide? Examine each factor that contributed to the results of the study. Weigh each carefully—one or two factors are bound to emerge as significant.

Analytical development requires a sharp, detail-minded writer. You can't overlook a single aspect with this M.O.D.: the potential mousetrap market, the people behind the product, the projected mouse population for the next decade, costs, competition, manufacturing plans—everything. You're searching for the critical factors that will mean success. Or failure.

As with all other M.O.D.'s, be conscious of your reader. Often companies use the analytical method for company growth reports intended for the public. Simplify in-company technical language to ensure easy readability.

USEFUL FOR: Technical reports, yearly overviews, analyses of trends, annual reports.

Choosing a method. To choose the M.O.D. that best suits your needs, start by asking yourself, "What method will be most appealing and helpful to my readers?" Consider your readers by asking:

Do they need to be persuaded?   *or*
Are they already in agreement with my viewpoint?

Which part of my message is most important?   *or*
Which is least important?

Do they need help understanding information?   *or*
Are they already familiar with the topic?

Are they looking for my opinion?   *or*
For a clear statement of research and facts only?

Do they need a neat summary?   *or*
In-depth analysis?

The summary question can be phrased two ways:

1. How will my readers relate to my thoughts?   *and*
2. How can I relate my thoughts to them?

Successful communication is successful *relating.* How well you relate to people depends on your position and theirs, too. Understanding your readers will help you position your ideas for greatest impact.

Other factors in your choice of M.O.D. Determining your readers' needs is not the only criterion for choosing your method of development. You will discover that certain types of writing just naturally lend themselves to a particular method. For example, how could you fail to choose a chronological M.O.D. if your report was entitled "From Minitrix, Inc., 1965, to Megatrix, Inc., 1984: How the Company Grew"?

As you can see, many of the M.O.D.'s explained in this chapter resemble each other. Combine as many as you need to create the structure that presents your material most clearly and, if necessary, persuasively.

⟳ ON YOUR OWN: Read over some old reports written by you or your colleagues to see if you can detect what M.O.D.'s they used. Label the different types in the margin. Was one method favored over others?

THE ORGANIZATION GAME

Here's a chance to apply what you've read about positioning your ideas. This game challenges your skill in organizing long proposals. On the following pages you will find a sixteen-page proposal presented in scrambled order. The text has been obscured to make you focus on the major concepts. The proposal recommends that a bank purchase a new penny-counting machine.

Your job: to arrange the pages in the most persuasive and coherent order. Assume your readers need to be persuaded but are not hostile to the proposal. Photocopy the pages, cut out each of the sixteen pages, and start organizing. Pay more attention to the beginning of the proposal than to the end. There are several correct ways to arrange the proposal, so don't expect to do it my way. Since the pages are alphabetized, you can list the pages by letter, below, in the order you choose.

1._____	5._____	9._____	13._____
2._____	6._____	10._____	14._____
3._____	7._____	11._____	15._____
4._____	8._____	12._____	16._____

How did you do? Compare the order you chose with my suggestions in Appendix A. I chose "most to least important" as my M.O.D. because it was not a controversial proposal. Is your sequence similar? Of course, there isn't just one correct answer; you needn't have chosen the exact order I chose—there are several possible ways to organize this or any report. However, you should have good reasons for each of your choices. In my solution I give you a few important issues to consider in organizing any report and my reasons for organizing the report as I did.

RECOMMENDATIONS FOR PURCHASE OF PENNY COUNTERS

F

(1) Install Penny Counting equipment in various departments of the Bank as indicated in the first two phases of the three phase implementation plan (pages ___ and ___. The equipment procured during Phase I and Phase II would replace all presently installed Penny Counters with 12 terminals and eight printers and also provide one VDT and one printer to the Management Planning Department. Phase I equipment as indicated in this report (page) represents the projected requirements subject to cost justification.

(2) Establish Zap Labs, Inc., as the standard vendor for all video display Penny Counting equipment procured by the Bank during the next three to five year period.

(3) Establish a schedule for the proposed staff reduction in relation to the equipment implementation. (This report proposes non-replacement of one clerk/typist in the Planning and Analysis Department, and reduction of typing staff by two persons, one in the Bank Supervision Division and another in the Research Department. (Section page)

(4) Approve the Penny Counting Equipment Procurement Guidelines proposed in this report. (Section page)

(5) Designate Planning and Analysis Department as central co-ordinator of all Penny Counting activities enumerated in this report. (Section Page)

(6) Select a standard typestyle for the typed material and Penny Counters to facilitate input of hard copy into the Penny Counter storage. Example of this appears on

---

PREDICTED PRODUCTIVITY IMPROVEMENTS

N

From the industry literature as well as method time measurement studies, we have determined that a productivity improvement of at least 3 percent is realistic in the Bank in view of the hardware and software features that would be available from the new Penny Counters.

TABLE OF CONTENTS

M

Reason for analysis	0
Scope of analysis	00
Background data	00
Equipment	00
Allocation cost	00
Penny Counter cost	30

ECONOMIC ADVANTAGES

O

Type of Budget	Present 1980 Budget	Revised 1982 Budget (includes Penny Counters)	Projected 1984 Budget
Capital Budget	$,700	$600	$6,000
Expense Budget (including New Equipment Depreciation)	$5,000	$400	$300

Expected Typing Personnel Saving: Three clerk/typists during 1982.

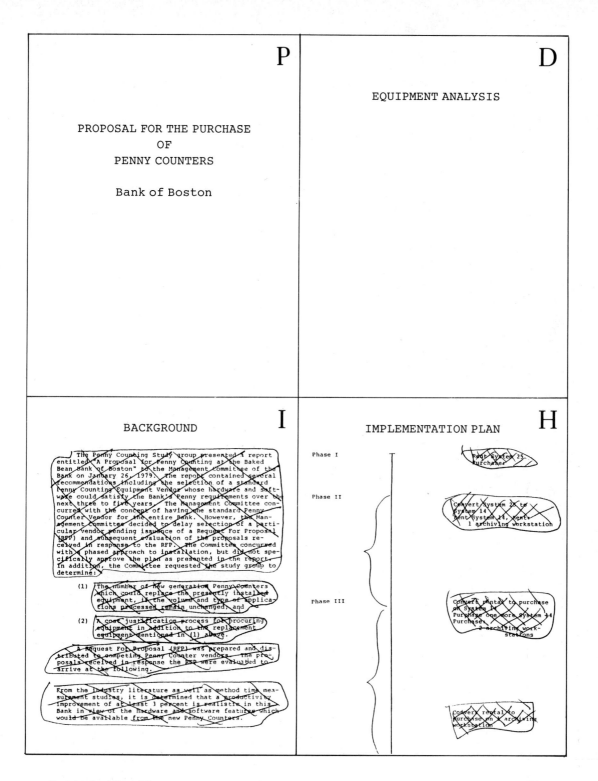

P

PROPOSAL FOR THE PURCHASE
OF
PENNY COUNTERS

Bank of Boston

D

EQUIPMENT ANALYSIS

I

BACKGROUND

The Penny Counting Study group presented a report entitled "A Proposal for Penny Counting at the Baked Bean Bank of Boston" to the Management Committee of the Bank on January 26, 1979. The report contained several recommendations including the selection of a standard Penny Counting Equipment Vendor whose hardware and software could satisfy the Bank's Penny requirements over the next three to five years. The Management Committee concurred with the concept of having one standard Penny Counter Vendor for the entire Bank. However, the Management Committee decided to delay selection of a particular vendor pending issuance of a Request For Proposal (RFP) and subsequent evaluation of the proposals received in response to the RFP. The Committee concurred with a phased approach to installation, but did not specifically approve the plan as presented in the report. In addition, the Committee requested the study group to determine:

(1) The number of new generation Penny Counters which could replace the presently installed equipment, if the volume and type of applications processed remain unchanged; and

(2) A cost justification process for procuring equipment in addition to the replacement equipment mentioned in (1) above.

A Request For Proposal (RFP) was prepared and distributed to competing Penny Counter vendors. The proposals received in response the RFP were evaluated to arrive at the following.

From the industry literature as well as method time measurement studies, it is determined that a productivity improvement of at least 3 percent is realistic in this Bank in view of the hardware and software features which would be available from the new Penny Counters.

H

IMPLEMENTATION PLAN

Phase I

Rent System 25 Purchase

Phase II

Convert System 25 to System 14 Rent System 14, rent 1 archiving workstation

Phase III

Convert rental to purchase on System Purchase one more System 14 Purchase 2 archiving workstations

Convert rental to purchase on 2 archiving workstation

K

FINAL SUMMARY

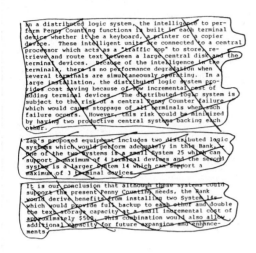

In a distributed logic system, the intelligence to perform Penny Counting functions is built in each terminal device whether it be a keyboard, a printer or a copier device. These intelligent units are connected to a central processor which acts as a "traffic cop" to store, retrieve and route text between a large central disk and the terminal devices. Because of the intelligence in the terminals, there is no performance degradation when several terminals are simultaneously operating. In a large installation, the distributed logic system provides cost saving because of low incremental cost of adding terminal devices. The distributed logic system is subject to the risk of a central Penny Counter failure which would cause stoppage of all terminals when such failure occurs. However, this risk would be minimized by having two productive central systems backing each other.

Zap's proposed equipment includes two distributed logic systems which would perform adequately in this Bank. One of the two systems is a small System 25 which can support a maximum of 4 terminal devices and the second system is a larger System 14 which can support a maximum of 3 terminal devices.

It is our conclusion that although these systems could support the present Penny Counting needs, the Bank would derive benefits from installing two System 14s which would provide full backup to each other and double the text storage capacity at a small incremental cost of approximately $500. This combination would also allow additional capacity for future expansion and enhancements

C

EQUIPMENT COST JUSTIFICATION

This equipment justification concerns only the equipment which would eventually replace the presently installed first generation equipment.

It should be noted that the cost comparison has a limited validity since the presently installed equipment may have to be scrapped prior to the five year comparison period even if some of the purchased items were overhauled during 19__ and 19__.

Cost Comparison
Present Versus Old-Time Penny Counters

Actual Annual Cost

End of Year	Investment in the New Equipment	Present 15 Typists	Old-Time 12 Typists	Annual Savings
0	$100			
1		$300	$500	$600
2		100	800	300
3		400	900	500
4		600	700	900
5		700	300	400
TOTAL	$100	$100	$200	$900

This cost comparison yields a payback period of approximately two years and three months.

It also gives an Internal Rate of Return on Investment equal to 3 percent assuming zero salvage value at the end of the five year period for both sets of equipment.

The net present value of the total dollar savings at seven percent discount is $600 and the net present value at nine percent discount is $600. Net present value equals present value of the savings at a discount factor less the initial investment.

J

IMPLEMENTATION TIMETABLE

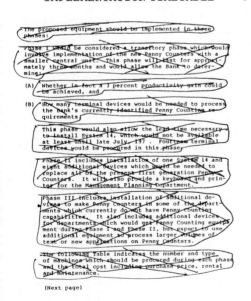

The proposed equipment should be implemented in three phases:

Phase I would be considered a transitory phase which could involve implementation of the new Penny Counters with a smaller central unit. This phase will last for approximately three months and would allow the Bank to determine:

(A) Whether in fact a 3 percent productivity gain could be achieved, and

(B) How many terminal devices would be needed to process the bank's currently identified Penny Counting requirements

This phase would also allow the lead time necessary to install System 14, which would not be available at least until late July, 197_. Fourteen terminal devices would be procured in this phase.

Phase II includes installation of one System 14 and eight additional devices which would be needed to replace all of the present first generation Penny Counters. It will also provide a keyboard and printer for the Management Planning Department.

Phase III includes installation of additional devices to make Penny Counters in some of the departments which currently do not have Penny Counting capabilities. It also includes additional devices for departments which would get Penny Counting equipment during Phase I and Phase II, but expect to use additional equipment to process larger volumes of text or new applications on Penny Counters.

The following Table indicates the number and type of machines which should be procured during each phase and the total cost including purchase price, rental and maintenance.

(Next page)

A

STAFFING REQUIREMENTS

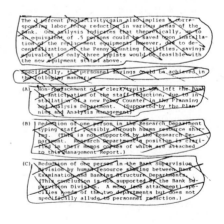

The 3 percent productivity gain also implies a corresponding labor force reduction in various areas of the Bank. Our analysis indicates that theoretically, up to an equivalent of .5 persons could be saved upon installation of the replacement equipment; however, due to decentralization of the Penny Counting facilities, savings equivalent to only three typists would be feasible with the new equipment stated above.

Specifically, the personnel savings could be achieved in the following manner:

(A) Non-replacement of a clerk/typist who left the Bank in anticipation of the staff reduction, due to installation of a new Penny Counter in the Planning and Analysis Department. (Supported by the Planning and Analysis Management)

(B) Reduction of one person in the Research Department typing staff, possibly through human resource sharing. (This is not supported by the Research Department. Research Department's position is clarified in their memos copies of which are attached to this Management Report.)

(C) Reduction of one person in the Bank Supervision Division by human resource sharing between Bank Examination and Banking Structure Departments. (This conclusion is not supported by the Bank Supervision Division. A memo [see attachment] specifies needs of the two departments but does not specifically allude to personnel reduction.)

EQUIPMENT DEPRECIATION

MANAGEMENT PLANNING DEPARTMENT

If it is assumed that the Management Planning Department would be able to avoid employing one person instead of .74 since fractional persons cannot be easily employed or reduced, the savings from cost avoidance would be as follows:

Year	Projected cost allocation due to equipment	Projected savings from manpower avoidance equal to one person	Net projected savings
May 1 - Dec. 31, 19__	$30	$700	$700
Jan. 1 - Dec. 31, 19__	$30	$300	$300
Total	$60	$9,000	$1,000

E

VENDOR AND
EQUIPMENT SELECTION

G

(1) Vendor Selection

Our analysis of the proposals submitted by vendors establishes Zap Laboratories, Inc. as the leading vendor. The five year total cost of $200 for Zap Labs minimum equipment which meets the requirements set forth in the RFP is the second lowest price available to the Bank. The lowest five year total cost available in $600. Superior service and training support as well as the availability of certain desirable features which are not available on the lowest cost alternative make Zap's proposed equipment the best alternative available to the Bank.

(2) Equipment Selection

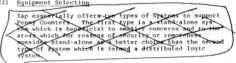

Zap essentially offers two types of systems to support Penny Counters. The first type is a stand-alone system which is beneficial to smaller concerns and to those areas which for reasons of security or remoteness consider stand-alone as a better choice than the second type of system which is termed a distributed logic system.

IMPLEMENTATION
CONSIDERATIONS

B

MANAGEMENT OVERVIEW
(ABSTRACT)

L

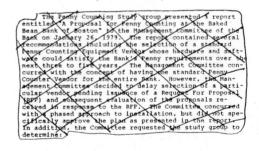

The Penny Counting Study group presented a report entitled "A Proposal for Penny Counting at the Baked Bean Bank of Boston" to the Management Committee of the Bank on January 26, 1979. The report contained several recommendations including the selection of a standard Penny Counting Equipment Vendor whose hardware and software could satisfy the Bank's Penny requirements over the next three to five years. The Management Committee concurred with the concept of having one standard Penny Counter Vendor for the entire Bank. However, the Management Committee decided to delay selection of a particular vendor pending issuance of a Request For Proposal (RFP) and subsequent evaluation of the proposals received in response to the RFP. The Committee concurred with a phased approach to installation, but did not specifically approve the plan as presented in the report. In addition, the Committee requested the study group to determine:

How I organized this report. I'm sure you started with the title page followed by the table of contents, as I did. The big issue is what comes next. I chose the "management overview." The "management overview" should always be placed before the body of the report. This section—sometimes called an "abstract" or a "preliminary summary"—is the key to a successful report, but unfortunately it is neglected by many writers. I cannot emphasize enough how essential it is for any memo or report of more than three pages to have a short, readable summary at the beginning to help readers get to the "bottom line" quickly. With an overview, the readers can skim the entire report, concentrating only on those details that are important to them.

Why this approach? Since the function of your report is to present your recommendations, it would be counterproductive to hide them in the last pages of a long report. It is to your advantage to place them at the beginning, where the reader can easily find them. Although you may find it unorthodox, I also took the liberty of placing "predicted productivity improvements" and "economic advantages" at the beginning of the report. These are persuasive arguments, and it's essential they be read if your point of view is to prevail. Your readers are busy people: if you don't convince them in the first few pages, they may not give you a second chance. Most managers only read the first few pages.

After presenting your recommendations and persuaders, continue to order the sections according to the most important to least important M.O.D. I decided "equipment analysis" was the next most important issue. If you disagreed, don't worry. The order of the elements from here on is not crucial, as long as it is sensible.

I'm sure you are surprised that "background" appears so late in the report. I did this to point out to you how often writers mistakenly give the background far too much attention. Whenever you present background information, ask yourself if it's really vital to the readers' understanding. If you discover yourself rehearsing a dull bit of history that most of your readers already know, move it to the end, as I did. Those who need to read it will. The summary at the end recaps your major goal and persuaders. It is your last opportunity to convince your readers. Use it!

A final word. Judge your success on this exercise only by how well you arranged the first six pages. After reading my solution, evaluate the reasoning behind your choices. With any memo or report designed to recommend something, your goal is to persuade the reader to accept your suggestions. Would your order have had the greatest possible impact on the reader? Remember, putting your "bottom line" at the top is usually the key.

5
Writing the
First Draft

Now that you have your well-ordered list of headlines, you're ready for the next step—the first draft. As you did with free writing, develop the ideas from your headline list. Write about them one at a time without regard to style or grammar. Be bold—put down what you're thinking, even if the sentences are messy and graceless. You can clean up your draft later. Remember, it's always easier to edit than to write.

Don't get hung up on that first, most difficult sentence. You can sit at your desk for hours—if you've got nothing better to do—worriedly rewriting your opener. But if that first sentence is not apparent right away, forget about it and get on with your writing. You can go back later, when the pressure is off, and put in the missing sentence. Some of the best beginnings have been written last—after you really understand what your intention was.

Headlines help you decide where to start. How can you best make use of your headlines? Headlines can help you decide which sections you'll tackle first—for, as professional writers know, you needn't necessarily write part one first. Maybe you're the type who prefers to get the easy material out of the way immediately. Or maybe you'll want to go after a difficult section right away because you feel alert and up to the challenge. In short, start with whatever section appeals to you.

Headlines can also give you clues for writing the tricky first sentence of a paragraph, known as the topic sentence. You might, for example, start writing a section headlined "Purpose" with these words: "The purpose of this memo . . ." Sound redundant? Don't worry. At least you've made a start. Later, you can go back and translate it into more original language.

REMEMBER: The topic (first) sentence of your paragraph should usually contain the most important information.

I want to stress that there are many ways to begin a first draft. The best approach is to jump in and do it. Get something—anything—down on paper.

The myth of the perfect first draft. Ed Itwell, like most people who are not professional writers, believed in a popular myth: that the skilled writer can create an excellent piece of writing—with commas and capitals in all the right places—in one swift draft. It's just plain NOT TRUE—whatever your favorite author says on talk shows.

The fact is, very few professional writers produce a perfect draft the first time around. F. Scott Fitzgerald's stories went through a minimum of five drafts before publication. And even after a writer has worked on a manuscript, it goes to a professional editor to be revised and polished.

People who believe that it's possible to write a perfect draft the first time probably think that's the way to save a lot of fuss. Instead, they usually find themselves facing paralysis and confusion because they are trying to do two things at once.

Content versus form. After the planning stages, the writing task consists of two very different activities: (1) creating content and (2) structuring the form. Generating content is a creative process during which all possibly useful ideas should be allowed to emerge. When you write your first draft, your approach should be like that of free writing—do not censor or edit yourself the first time through, no matter how outrageous or silly or stupid you may sound. Working on form means being your own critic—that should happen much later.

Divide the process into two steps. Remember this important distinction:

DRAFT 1: Work on content: express all your ideas and research in rough sentences or phrases as quickly as possible; let the ideas flow; try to keep the momentum going.

DRAFT 2: Work on form after you've expressed all possible content: rewrite to improve sentence structure, word choice, paragraph coherence and all the other editing tasks covered in part two of this book.

If you try to work on content and form at the same time, it will most likely slow you down. These two activities require such different brain functions that it's extremely frustrating to switch back and forth. For example, if in the middle of the first draft you stop for five minutes to grope for the perfect word, you'll no doubt lose your train of thought and grind to a halt. Leave a space where the word belongs and fill it in later.

Wait until all your ideas are on paper before polishing and refining your writing. It will save time in the long run. It only breaks your concentration if you try to edit each sentence as you write it.

Professional writers usually ask each other, "What draft are you on?" Dividing the writing process into two steps will ultimately save you time. Try it. One good way to start your first draft is to write with a time limit. The ticking clock may prevent you from daydreaming. Use the free-writing approach to fill this page as quickly as you can. This time do not allow your thoughts to wander; stick to ideas you've developed from any one of the Start-Up Strategies.

Writing the First Draft

Directions: Fill in the blank below marked "Start Time" with the time you begin. Write down your thoughts on "why I deserve a promotion," or on any other topic developed from your work with this book. Use additional paper if you need to. When you're finished, fill in the time you stopped in the second blank, marked "Finish Time," at the bottom of the page.

START TIME: _____

Why I Deserve a Promotion (or other title)

FINISH TIME: _____

Your approach to the first draft influences your speed. How long did it take you? If it took you more than five minutes to fill the page, you may be approaching your first draft incorrectly. You should be able to write down several ideas quickly, even if they are roughly worded. If you filled only half the page, you were probably worrying too much about word choice or sentence construction. The myth of the perfect first draft again! Try the exercise once more, and *don't* edit yourself as you go.

If you filled the page in five minutes or under, you're doing well. Here are more suggestions for making the writing process easier.

Paragraphs. A well-constructed paragraph is composed of a group of ideas that tend to fall together under a given headline. Traditionally each paragraph begins with a topic sentence that expresses the main thought of the paragraph. Using a headline emphasizes the crucial topic sentence even further by introducing it or stating it in a different and appealing way. There is no right or wrong size to a paragraph. Like the sentences that compose them, paragraphs should be flexible in size, structure and emphasis. Variety holds the reader's attention. But in every effective paragraph the sentences should support and extend one another to form a single developing idea.

A simple rule to remember: one paragraph, one thought.

To be sure you can determine where one idea begins and another ends, try the next exercise.

Paragraphs

Directions: Indicate where new paragraphs should begin.*

In 1980, the United States faced what was believed to be an acute shortage of lunar rock analysis engineers that was predicted to get worse over the next decade. The 1981 Technology Training Act authorized substantial federal funds to increase the training of these high-technology professionals. Universe University was one of fifteen space-shot engineering schools to compress its four-year curriculum into three years in order to train more astroengineers in a shorter time. Class size quickly jumped from 135 to 190 to meet special federal funding requirements. The capacity to respond to changing professional and societal needs is incumbent upon leading institutions such as Universe University. In 1925, Universe University's Engineering School was one of the first in the nation to adopt the five-year curriculum so that new courses, and a more intensive presentation of old ones, could be provided. Now that the lunar rock analysis engineering manpower crisis has passed, schools across the country are returning to pre-1980 curricula. Universe University has readopted its previous four-year format. All aspects of the school's educational and extracurricular programing will be back to normal until our next successful space probe.

*Answer appears on pages 133–34.

One idea per paragraph. If you have difficulty knowing where your paragraphs should begin or end, you are probably having trouble separating one idea from another. It should be possible to sum up the sentences in a paragraph into one conclusive sentence. A headline condenses this idea even further.

If you think you're writing about just one idea but you can't really explain it in one sentence, your paragraph will reflect your uncertainty. By forcing yourself to create a headline for every paragraph, you will eliminate vagueness in your thoughts as well as in your words. Then, even if you remove some of the headlines in the final draft, each paragraph will clearly express a single idea.

REMEMBER: Always limit the content of any paragraph to one idea, labeled by a headline.

WHEN YOU'RE STUCK

You've followed all the instructions thus far but you're still overwhelmed and confused. Somehow you've gotten off the track—but where? Let's review.

Ask yourself:
- Do I really understand my task? my objective?
- Have I defined the topic correctly?
- Have I analyzed my audience well enough?
- Am I trying to attack a topic that's simply too big?
- Do I really have all the information I need?
- Have I gathered too many facts; too few?
- Am I organizing my facts in the best way?
- Have I broken my writing job into manageable subtasks?
- Have I decided in which order to complete the subtasks?
- Have I allowed myself enough time to meet my deadline?
- Do I have a work schedule that I'm sticking to?
- Is my environment too distracting?
- At what point in the process am I stuck?
  —knowing my objective
  —analyzing the audience
  —gathering information by using a Start-Up Strategy or fact-finding
  —analyzing the information
  —choosing a Method of Development
  —writing the first draft
  —editing and revising

Still having trouble?

Try the rewriting strategy. Sometimes your letter or memo (or paragraph) just doesn't sound right. You've rearranged phrases, changed words, and added so many inserts and arrows that you yourself can't read it anymore.

In this situation it may be more efficient simply to put away your draft and start again. Words are not precious; there are plenty more where the first ones came from. The Nobel Prize-winning writer Isaac Bashevis Singer calls the wastebasket "the writer's best friend."

⌕ ON YOUR OWN: Quickly write a one-page memo on any topic. After you've finished, fold it up and start again. Don't look at the first one. Repeat the process a second time. Now compare the three drafts. Chances are you'll prefer a later draft. Why?

Suggested topic:

You recently interviewed Mr. Paul Tree for an important position in your department. You think he'd be great for the job, but you've heard he's about to take a position elsewhere. In a letter, offer him the position and try to convince him that this is his best choice.

This rewriting strategy is designed to prove that rewriting can be as efficient as revising when you're stuck. Take the strategy seriously. For some frustrated managers, rewriting has dramatically changed their ability to get past the tough spots. Professional writers use it constantly. Try it enough times to give it a chance to work.

What to do when you're so blocked that you're desperate. The Beatles had the right idea when they sang, "I get by with a little help from my friends." When all else fails, look around for someone with a bit of extra time who's willing to help you out. Tell the person that you're struggling with writer's block and that talking over your writing project would help you tremendously. Ask your helper to listen to you carefully and ask questions whenever he or she feels the need for clarification.

Bring along a tape recorder and tape the conversation. Use the Start-Up Sheet as a guide for the conversation. Mention every possible idea and bit of information you're thinking of including—you can always delete extraneous material later. After your conversation, play the tape back and take notes on Post-It Note Tape or, if it's a long report, on 3×5 index cards. Add any other information that has occurred to you in the meantime. After putting your ideas in the best order, you're ready to start the first draft.

Note: You can use this approach without a tape recorder if either (or both) of you takes notes as you talk.

A different approach to beating writer's block

(1) Change environments—find a quiet place with no distractions.

(2) Ask a co-worker to take a look at your work. Outside suggestions help.

(3) Make a checklist of tasks that you still must complete. Check them off so you can *see* your progress.

(4) Skip to another section that you know you can write.

(5) Take a break. Leave it for a while. Get up and stretch. Walk around. Jog. Dance. Get distance. Come back to the job refreshed, with a positive attitude.

Getting distance. Try to finish your writing enough ahead of time to allow a rest period. Put it away for a day or so and forget about it. When you're too involved, too close to your work, it's difficult to recognize your mistakes. You want the last review of your writing to be as objective as possible before you send it out. Even an hour can be enough to distance yourself from your earlier deep immersion in your ideas. For example, you may think you wrote perfectly clear instructions for your assistant to purchase a new computer printer. Upon reviewing, you discover that you failed to specify that he should arrange an installment plan for payment —a potentially costly mistake. Put enough time between writing and reviewing so that it will seem that someone else wrote the material. It's easy to pick out other people's errors or omissions—and so hard to see one's own.

HOW TO WRITE A PROBLEM-SOLVING MEMO

No wonder you're stuck! You're trying to solve a thorny problem on paper and write a memo, too. To accomplish both, you must marshal analytical skills, as well as creativity and imagination. Let's go through the process step by step.

To write a problem-solving memo, first analyze the situation—on paper—and then reorganize your analysis into an effective format.

Planning the memo

STEP 1: On a sheet of paper, write a description of the problem you face. List symptoms (evidence of the problem) on a second piece of paper. For example, a high rate of employee turnover may turn out to be the symptom of a larger problem. By listing the symptoms, you may discover the larger problem. Perhaps it is competition among employers, a lack of advancement opportunities or frustration over working conditions. Restate the problem if the symptoms have given it another form.

STEP 2: On a third sheet, list causes of the problem. What preceded or caused the situation? Contributing factors may be economic, historic, environmental or social. Mention any important background material here.

STEP 3: Propose several solutions to the problem. Use the Brainstorm Outline strategy (page 19) to help you create as many solutions to your problem as possible. Be daring; put any and all ideas you have onto the page. When you are looking for solutions, ignore your internal critic. This step should help you avoid jumping to conclusions or overlooking possibilities.

STEP 4: List strengths and weaknesses of each solution, taking causes into account.

STEP 5: Choose one of the solutions and summarize the reasons for your choice. If you really can't figure out the solution, don't be afraid to say so. Perhaps your solution should be to request a brainstorm session to enlist the advice of others.

Evaluate what you have so far

STEP 6: Does your solution make sense? Are there hidden issues surrounding the problem that will invalidate what you've decided? Have you really considered the limitations that might weaken your solution, such as budget, space limits or staffing requirements?

STEP 7: How will your boss or the reader of your memo react to your solution? If you expect negativity, how will you counter it? The ideas you generate here are your persuaders. They should appear toward the beginning of your memo.

STEP 8: If your memo concerns a situation you are negotiating, decide in advance: (a) What do you really want? (b) What is the least you'd accept? (c) What would really convince your reader in your favor? (d) Have you included these among your persuaders?

STEP 9: Write a short summary of your memo, reminding the reader of your best solution. Refer again to your persuaders if you can do so briefly.

Writing the memo

1. Reorganize your plan for impact. You should structure the memo this way:
   A. (1) Problem
   B. (5) Recommended solution
   C. (7, 8) Persuaders—why your solution is the right one
   D. (2) Background
      • Causes
      • Symptoms (You may mention these briefly in the problem section.)
   E. (3) Alternative solutions
      • Pros/strengths
      • Cons/weaknesses

F. (9) Summary
(*Note:* The numbers in parentheses on the outline correspond to the sections you wrote in "planning the memo.")

2. Write your draft in clear, concise sentences and paragraphs.
3. Use headlines.
4. Edit.
5. Revise/proofread.

A SAMPLE PROBLEM-SOLVING MEMO

TO: Jack Bolt

FROM: Lee King, Maintenance Supervisor

RE: Water pump failure at Boston plant

Problem
The repeated breakdown of the outboard cooling water pump has brought the company to the brink of shutdown one more time. This situation must be corrected, and it's been impossible to reach you by phone.

Recommended solution
My investigation into the problem reveals that the impeller is out of balance. The impeller should be disassembled and sent back to the manufacturer for balancing and additional testing.

Why this is the best solution
We haven't tried sending the impeller back to the manufacturer yet. It should be our first solution because it's the cheapest and could solve the problem.

The failure of this pump leaves us with only the auxiliary pump to handle the required water flow. When the auxiliary is in use, we have no backup pump. If we were to lose the auxiliary pump, the plant would have to be shut down. The loss of this plant for any length of time would be measured in lost profit.

Background
This particular pump supplies water to the three main heat exchangers of the plant. It was purchased from Apex Pump

(continued)

Company and was installed by Jones Bros. Construction Company eighteen months ago. Yesterday, the pump broke down for the fourth time since it was put into service.

I personally disassembled the pump and could see no other problem but this one. All the failures have caused the same specific damage to the bearings: they become badly scarred and worn. Operators say the pump has always been noisy, and Maintenance says vibration readings have always been abnormally high.

Other solutions considered but rejected
1. Buy a whole new pump—too expensive.
2. Buy a new impeller. In talks with the pump manufacturer, I was told that we would have to wait 8-10 weeks for delivery of a new impeller. This is too long to wait. Also, the replacement cost for a new unit is substantially higher than what we paid eighteen months ago, and much more than it would cost to have the impeller rebalanced.
3. Bring in another expert to look at the pump. Jack, you might want to do this for your own peace of mind, but I sincerely feel that my judgment is right and that any expert would agree. Why waste more time and money?

Summary
This problem is pressing, but I think we can solve it soon. I'll send the impeller to the manufacturer as soon as you give me the go-ahead. Meanwhile, I'll keep trying to reach you by phone.

6
Writing to Persuade

Psyching out your readers. Whenever you begin writing, ask yourself several questions about your readers. The answers will determine how you present your message. The more you know about your readers, the better your chances of getting the response you want.

- Are your readers open to your ideas?
- Are they likely to be supportive or skeptical?
- Do you know them personally?
- How familiar are they with your topic?
- Will they understand your technical language?
- How informal can you be?
- If you are suggesting a change, how disconcerting will it be to them?
- What readability level should you use? (See chapter 7.)

Choose the correct tone. Knowing the answers to the preceding questions will help you to reach out to your readers. The answers will determine not only the order of your ideas, but also the best tone to adopt. Choose your words to fit your readers' personality and background. You already change the way you talk depending on the company; why not do the same in your writing?

Compare the tone of these two report titles:

"Benefits of Acquiring the XLC Multicopier at Teletrix, Inc."

"How the Purchase of the XLC Multicopier Would Save Time, Money and Energy at Teletrix, Inc."

In the first one, the tone is remote and abstract. The tone of the second title is more lively and reflects an awareness that the reader is one of the decision-makers on the issue.

When you have a choice, be friendly and informal. Business writing is changing in the direction of informality and straightforwardness. The friendlier and more "real" you sound, the better chance you have of relating to your reader. Be formal only when you feel it's unavoidable. Modernize your language by avoiding stuffy sentences like, "Should you require further assistance, please do not hesitate to write to my attention."

As Winston Churchill said, "The short words are best. . . ." The following list shows some modern alternatives to the worn-out words and phrases that sound so pretentious today:

Instead of:	Use:	Instead of:	Use:
initiate, commence	begin, start	we would like to ask that you	please
nevertheless	but	for the reason that	because
terminate	end	are of the opinion	believe
utilize	use	for the purpose of	for, to
deem	think	prior to	before
assistance	help	despite the fact that	although, though
converse	talk	in view of the fact that	because, since
forward	send, mail	in order to	to
advise	tell	in the amount of	for
indicate	show	subsequent to	after
procure	get	with respect (or reference to	about
reside	live	on the occasion of	when
		during the course of	during
		along the lines of	like
		succeed in making	make
		make use of	use
		have need for	need
		give consideration to	consider

Tautologies. When you use a tautology you're repeating yourself unnecessarily. Watch out for the following redundancies:

advanced ahead	final ending
attached hereto	hopeful optimism
at this point in time	important essentials
basic fundamentals	in the same way as described
brief in duration	just exactly
both together	merge together
cooperate together	mutual cooperation
enclosed herein	necessary requisite

one a.m. in the morning	seems apparent
plan in advance	surrounding circumstances
protrude out	still continue
reduce down	true facts
resume again	ultimate end
round in shape	young juveniles

Detecting excessive formality in letters. There are many things wrong with this letter, but the big problem is that it's too formal. Circle all the words or phrases that should be changed or eliminated to improve the tone of the letter.

January 23, 1982

Skip Sempleton
Manufacturer's Representative
Fogg Smoke Warning Systems
7734 Rodeo Drive
Los Angeles, CA 96234

Dear Mr. Sempleton:

   I wish to thank you for your prompt reply to my urgent letter of last week depicting the grave situation at hand. As you are no doubt aware, it is an absolute necessity for the safety of our patients and our entire staff to have an extensive and dependable smoke warning system. Because of the inavailability of your customary repairman, Mr. Al S. Besto, we are compelled to hire a nonwarranteed service firm. To be sure, an ounce of prevention is worth a pound of cure.

   As you requested, I am forwarding a list of the rooms where the breakdowns occur most frequently. I am also enclosing a copy of the hospital floor plan, upon which I have noted the areas experiencing different types of breakdowns. Note: In some rooms (circled in red) the alarms ring at twenty-minute intervals, certainly not conducive to the healing atmosphere of a hospital.

   Also, another problem has arisen since we last corresponded. On several smoke detectors, the flashing

(continued)

---

light that is supposed to accompany the alarm lights up independently from said alarm. This has had particularly distressing consequences in Ward E, where countless patients have complained about flashing lights disturbing them late at night. It is expected that you will find this situation as intolerable as we do. At this point in time, no other flaws appear to exist.

Lastly, with respect to the warranty. Clearly, we cannot wait for Mr. Besto to repair the smoke warning system, since he is hopelessly busy. Although I am aware that the Fogg policy normally covers expenses only when the repair work is done by our dealer—i.e., Mr. Besto—I presume that the policy will be relaxed in this disturbing circumstance, allowing us to engage an alternative firm. Would you be so kind as to clarify this in writing?

I trust that you will contact me pursuant to these pressing issues at your earliest convenience. Your assistance is greatly appreciated.

Very truly yours,

Hiram Frost
Vice-President
Physical Plant Safety

How did you do? Compare your responses with those below. Did you pick out most of the problem areas?

January 23, 1982

Skip Sempleton
Manufacturer's Representative
Fogg Smoke Warning Systems
7734 Rodeo Drive
Los Angeles, CA 96234

Dear Mr. Sempleton:

I (wish) to thank you for your prompt reply to my urgent letter of last week (depicting) the (grave situation at hand.)

As you are no doubt aware, it is an absolute necessity for the safety of our patients and our entire staff to have an extensive and dependable smoke warning system. Because of the inavailability of your customary repairman, Mr. Al S. Besto, we are compelled to hire a nonwarranteed service firm. To be sure, an ounce of prevention is worth a pound of cure.

As you requested, I am forwarding a list of the rooms where the breakdowns occur most frequently. I am also enclosing a copy of the hospital floor plan, upon which I have noted the areas experiencing different types of breakdowns. Note: In some rooms (circled in red) the alarms ring at twenty-minute intervals, certainly not conducive to the healing atmosphere of a hospital.

Also, another problem has arisen since we last corresponded. On several smoke detectors, the flashing light that is supposed to accompany the alarm lights up independently from said alarm. This has had particularly distressing consequences in Ward E, where countless patients have complained about flashing lights disturbing them late at night. It is expected that you will find this situation as intolerable as we do. At this point in time, no other flaws appear to exist.

Lastly, with respect to the warranty. Clearly, we cannot wait for Mr. Besto to repair the smoke warning system, since he is hopelessly busy. Although I am aware that the Fogg policy normally covers expenses only when the repair work is done by our dealer—i.e., Mr. Besto—I presume that the policy will be relaxed in this disturbing circumstance, allowing us to engage an alternative firm. Would you be so kind as to clarify this in writing?

I trust that you will contact me pursuant to these pressing issues at your earliest convenience. Your assistance is greatly appreciated.

Very truly yours,

Hiram Frost
Vice-President
Physical Plant Safety

Now try rewriting the letter yourself in a friendly and informal tone. Change or remove pompous, old-fogy phrases while retaining as much of the meaning as possible.

Here's my version of the Fogg letter. How does it compare with yours?

January 23, 1982

Skip Sempleton
Manufacturer's Representative
Fogg Smoke Warning System
7734 Rodeo Drive
Los Angeles, CA 96234

RE: Immediate O.K. needed for smoke detector repair

Dear Mr. Sempleton:

   Thank you for your quick reply to my urgent letter of December 18, 1982. As you know, the safety of our patients and staff depend upon an extensive and dependable smoke warning system. The system you sold us breaks down often and must be repaired immediately, even if it means our hiring a nonwarranteed service firm. Our dealer, Mr. Al S. Besto, is too busy to take the job.

   As you requested, I am sending you a list of rooms where the breakdowns occur most frequently. I am also enclosing a copy of the hospital floor plan, upon which I have noted areas of breakdown. Rooms circled in red have alarms that ring at twenty-minute intervals.

   Another problem has come up since I last wrote to you. The flashing light on several smoke detectors goes on independently of the alarm. In Ward E, patients have complained of flashing lights disturbing them late at night. This situation is, of course, unacceptable to us.

   One last word about the warranty. Since our problems are so urgent, we cannot wait for our dealer, Mr. Besto, to repair the smoke warning system. His time is booked solid for the next several weeks. While I am aware that the Fogg policy normally covers expenses only for work performed by Mr. Besto, I sincerely hope that the policy will be relaxed in our case to permit us to hire another service firm. We will assume you'll relax it unless we are informed in writing by next week.

   Thank you in advance for your help.

Sincerely,

Hiram Frost
Vice-President
Physical Plant Safety

How I rewrote the Fogg letter

- It is important that you write in a down-to-earth manner using, as often as possible, words that imply action. You must state everything you intend, for, above all, you want the recipient of your letter to know exactly what action you expect.
- Putting the header RE: below the inside address helps introduce the reader to the situation.
- The first paragraph was rewritten to eliminate unnecessary words, to state clearly the problem and the desired action, and to enable Sempleton to easily find your last letter in his files.
- In paragraph two, I have cut out some unnecessary words and deleted that "Note"—it did not seem to add to the meaning of the sentence.
- Paragraph three was reworded to take out redundancies, pompous words ("said"), overstatement ("countless") and useless words ("At this point in time").
- Paragraph four was streamlined by taking out theatrical words ("hopelessly," "in this disturbing circumstance") and by clarifying the action requested.
- There is no need to ask Sempleton to "contact me pursuant to these issues" in the last paragraph since that request was already made in the previous paragraph. I changed the note of thanks from passive voice to active for greater impact.

Adopting a modern tone. Fifty years ago, a formal tone was proper for business letters and memos. Today, the polite formality of the past is often taken for coldness or snobbishness. If, for example, you are writing to ask for someone's help, you don't want to sound distant. It is better to use the lighter and friendlier words of your daily speech.

On the facing page are two memos written by an office supervisor asking for help from her employees in solving a problem. Which one do you think will receive a better response?

I'm sure you agree that the second memo is far more likely to result in an amicable solution to the problem than the first. The second uses warmth and understanding to mobilize group spirit. The well-chosen tone shows that the writer understands how to motivate people. In the final sentence, she sets positive expectations, thus increasing the likelihood that her staff will cooperate.

Is Your Writing Too Formal? Let's see how skilled you are at translating formal words into down-to-earth ones. On page 82 is a list of thirty-eight inflated words. In many cases, it would be far better to use a simpler word. Fill in each blank using a more direct word with the same meaning.*

*For answers, see page 134.

Issues We All Face

```
TO:    Sinutrix Staff
FROM: Bea Bland
RE:    Smoking in the office

There has been great concern expressed about the growing
ill feelings between the office personnel who smoke and
those who do not. The most pressing issue at hand is
discerning if a reorganization of the office, based on
smoking preferences, is necessary.

Since this developing tension between smokers and
nonsmokers has great potential for unsettling the office
and reducing worker productivity, it must be addressed
without further delay. Kindly submit any suggestions
deemed suitable to the shift supervisor. This matter is of
concern to all.
```

```
TO:    Sinutrix Staff
FROM: Bea Bland
RE:    Smoking in the office

I'm becoming very concerned about the growing tension
between smokers and nonsmokers that threatens to make our
office a less pleasant place to work. Perhaps we should
consider reorganizing the office to improve the
atmosphere between the two groups.

Since this is a problem that affects us all, why not take a
minute to submit any suggestions you might have for
improving the situation. If we all put our heads together,
surely we can come up with a solution that will meet
everyone's needs. Thank you in advance for your
cooperation.
```

1. to anticipate _____	20. in the event that _____
2. to appear _____	21. to locate _____
3. to ascertain _____	22. per _____
4. to assist _____	23. personnel _____
5. to cooperate _____	24. pertaining to _____
6. to deem _____	25. presently _____
7. to desire _____	26. prior to _____
8. to determine _____	27. to prohibit _____
9. to disclose _____	28. to request _____
10. to effect _____	29. to require _____
11. to endeavor _____	30. residence _____
12. to ensue _____	31. to reveal _____
13. to execute _____	32. to review _____
14. to forward _____	33. spouse _____
15. to furnish _____	34. to state _____
16. inasmuch as _____	35. sufficient _____
17. to indicate _____	36. to supply _____
18. initial _____	37. to terminate _____
19. in lieu of _____	38. to transpire _____

Which letter is more persuasive? The letters on pages 83 and 84 were written by two account executives from different advertising companies. Each was trying to convince the Blippo Computer company to contract with her company for an ad campaign. Read each one through and decide which tone you feel is more persuasive. Then fill out the response sheet below:

Marketing Letters Response Sheet

1. Which letter do you think was more persuasive?

2. List four words describing the first letter.

3. List four words describing the second letter.

4. On whom does the writer focus in the opening of letter 1?

5. On whom does the writer focus in the opening of letter 2?

VAN SNOOT ADVERTISING AGENCY
4321 Foply Boulevard
Boston, Massachusetts 02215

January 31, 1984

Mr. Willy Dewitt
Product Development
Blippo Computer
1234 Via Mallorca
San Diego, CA 94654

Dear Mr. Dewitt:

Having had a great deal of experience working on advertisements suitable for the computer industry, my company, Van Snoot Advertising Agency, desires to inform you as to the optimum methods for the planning and execution of a successful advertising campaign.

In the past we have been able to assist other computer companies lacking the expertise or the facilities to create an advertising campaign to successfully reach their intended market. Most companies are of course aware of the successful campaigns we have developed in the past and of the prestige associated with the Van Snoot Advertising Agency, but a brochure describing our team approach to advertising design will be found enclosed.

It is expected that this proposal will be of interest to you, and that we can arrange an interview with you soon.

We look forward to meeting you.

Very truly yours,

Ruth X. Van Snoot
Account Executive

RXVS:AFM

GOODMAN ADVERTISING AGENCY
10 Hartley Avenue
Boston, Massachusetts 02117

February 2, 1984

Mr. Willy Dewitt
Product Development
Blippo Computer
1234 Via Mallorca
San Diego, CA 94654

Dear Mr. Dewitt:

Your personal computer, the XL90, is an important
addition to the family of fine quality Blippo computers
already improving the lives of its users. But without a
well-planned and carefully executed advertising
campaign, the XL90 may fail to reach its entire potential
market.

My company, Goodman Advertising Agency, is one of the
oldest and most successful agencies in the country. Our
experienced and talented team of marketing research
analysts, graphic artists and writers are skilled in
developing the finest campaign for each product they
handle. I would appreciate the opportunity to meet with
you and discuss how our team may be of unique service to
you.

May I suggest June 5 at 2:00 P.M.?

Cordially,

Alice Goodman
Account Executive

AG:AFM

6. Which approach is more likely to involve and engage the reader?

7. Which closing is more likely to result in a meeting? Why?

   On page 134 are my answers to the response sheet. Compare yours to mine. Pay special attention to the answer to question 7. Try to adopt similar closing methods for your letters. They work!

The positive approach. Sometimes your tone carries a hidden message to the reader. You must be aware of whether you are communicating, between the lines, your self-confidence or your self-doubt to the reader. Ideas expressed positively are most likely to be positively received by the reader. To get the results you desire, you must convey an attitude of confident expectation.

Avoid "no" and "not." Some people are always cheerful, self-assured and optimistic. They express themselves positively, both orally and in writing. The rest of us tend to express ourselves more negatively. And most of the time we don't even notice how negative we sound. But if, like me, you tend to write "Do not waste energy" instead of "Conserve energy," then you, too, are taking a negative approach.

   "Don't take a negative approach!" is my message to you, but it would be better to say, "Accentuate the positive." It is always more persuasive to suggest what you want than what you don't want.

   In the space provided on the following page, rewrite the negative sentences in a more positive style. When you're finished, turn to page 134 to compare your changes with mine.

The Positive Approach

   Directions: Rewrite the following sentences to express these thoughts in a more positive way.

   1. We hope you will not be disappointed with the results.
   2. Without proper planning we will not be able to prevent overcrowding.
   3. We are sorry, but we cannot process your order until you have paid the balance on your account.
   4. What an ugly baby!
   5. No doubt the changes should prove worthwhile.
   6. Not to provide this information is intolerable.
   7. If nothing goes wrong we will know that we have not been mistaken.
   8. The results of his research made no insignificant contribution to our final decision.

9. Do not ignore details; they are not unimportant.

10. This job is going to be nearly impossible to do.

👁‍🗨 ON YOUR OWN: Look over some of your recent letters and memos to see if you suffer from "the negative approach." If you find an abundance of *no*s and *not*s, they could be a signal. Watch for this weakness in future writing.

7
Are You Communi- cating?

NEGOTIATIONS AND STRATEGIES

Bargaining. More and more often we find ourselves negotiating on paper for the things we want: the right salary and benefits package for a new job, a preliminary commitment from a potential client or even a palimony agreement. Whenever you are involved in this sort of give and take, remember one old rule of thumb: always ask for more concessions than you really want.

Regardless of how much you like or respect the person you are negotiating with, you must respect yourself enough to win the concessions that matter to you —concessions that will ensure your sense of a fair negotiation. If you bargain only about the issues that you truly want to win, you're bound to lose a few of them: bargaining *means* trading off some of what you want in the expectation that the other person will do the same. When you ask for ten concessions, you are likely to end up with the five that really matter to you. If you start out asking for only the five items you truly want, you have nothing left to bargain with. A happy win-win situation is most likely to result if you begin negotiations with a few requests that you know can be thrown away if necessary.

Creating a win-win situation. Whenever you're negotiating, whether verbally or in writing, try to take a positive, win-win approach. By this I mean offering enough concessions so that both you and your "opposition" can win. This goal is particu- larly important in large corporations where you are constantly negotiating with the same people.

It may be easy to "blow your opponent out of the water" using a powerfully foxy strategy, but if you must face the same person or group a week later on a different issue, or if you must work side by side after the smoke clears, plan in advance what you can offer to create a situation where each side feels happy with the outcome. As a newly promoted manager, you may have only one chance to learn this lesson. Success is not always to the strongest.

Stalling for time. Sometimes you can use people's dislike of the writing process to gain time for yourself. Here's how one busy vice-president named Frank did it:

One day Frank was approached by an enthusiastic but misguided manager with a suggestion for improving the department. The suggestion seemed unworkable, and Frank was hopelessly busy the moment the manager chose to make his proposal.

Frank's reply? "Put it in writing, please. And then we'll talk." This was a good response to the situation because it forced the manager to think out his ideas more clearly (and to present them in the best possible light). It gave Frank time to ponder the unlikely idea a bit, avoiding an immediate negative reply that could discourage the manager if it seemed too hasty.

Executives often use their subordinates' dislike of writing to maneuver around dealing with unwanted suggestions. Many proposals have died a natural death when their originators felt it was just too much trouble to put it in writing. Asking that any verbal negotiation be documented will usually slow down the entire process and give you more time to plan your response.

Letters of agreement. You've reached a verbal understanding with someone and now it's time to put it into a letter for both of you to review. Having negotiated successfully this far, you may feel that the final cleverness would be to somehow maneuver the other party into writing the letter of agreement. Resist this temptation. It's wrong.

By writing the letter yourself you retain more power over the situation. The subtleties of the agreement will be construed in your favor, and any issues that remain in doubt will appear from your point of view. On the other hand, if you leave the agreement-writing to the other person, you are much more likely to be in the weak position of having to renegotiate points that were misunderstood by the writer or left out completely, intentionally or not. You'll be much happier with the results of any negotiation if you can reserve the writing of the agreement letter for yourself.

Carbon copies. David Ewing, an executive editor at the *Harvard Business Review,* asked a top executive for the most important step people might take to improve their written communications. The emphatic reply: "Not writing them at all!"*

Everyone agrees that since the advent of the Xerox machine many managers

*David Ewing, *Writing for Results* (New York: John Wiley & Sons, 1974), p. 17.

Issues We All Face

have been "carboned" to death with copies of memos having only the most remote relevance to them, but sent nevertheless by some well-intentioned soul. Avoid circulating copies of memos unless they really matter to each person receiving them. People will start ignoring your memos if they are merely courtesy copies.

With that caveat let's consider a few strategies for carbon copying.

1. The Hidden Warning

Managers often want to warn a few employees about unsatisfactory performance—being late for work, for example. Frequently these managers send a memo warning everybody concerned—guilty or not—because they are trying to avoid directly confronting the offending parties.

It is infuriating and demoralizing to receive a reprimand meant for someone else, particularly when you know *you* are innocent. Don't insult valued employees this way. Instead, deal with the offenders individually. If for some unlikely reason this seems impossible, start your memo with an apology such as, "I know that most of you are extremely punctual and I appreciate it more than you can imagine; however, a few of you . . ."

2. The Cowardly Warning

Some managers send warnings on paper because they find face-to-face encounters too upsetting to handle. If you're this type of manager, ask yourself these questions before committing yourself to paper:

(a) How will your subordinate feel about getting a warning on paper? Will it solve the situation or just prolong it?

(b) Will the subordinate want a chance to present his or her own side of the story? If so, you will end up facing the person anyway, so why not begin there?

(c) Do you really want this warning to be preserved on paper? Some things are better worked out verbally. A written chronicle of the problem may worsen the situation; well-meaning phrases can easily be misinterpreted as offensive by anyone wanting to take offense.

3. The Mystery Warning

Have you ever gotten a carbon-copied memo from a writer in your company whom you don't even know? Of course, this only happens in large corporations. Don't instantly dismiss a memo like this by assuming that it came from some blunderer suffering from Xerox mania. It is possible that such a memo could mean:

(a) There's someone new evaluating you or your colleagues.

(b) You or your department has done something serious enough to attract the attention of top management. Watch out.

(c) Someone is making a power play that could affect you in some way.

(d) Someone wants your job.

(e) Someone mistakenly thinks that you have more authority than you do. Perhaps you do have more than you think. Test it.

4. Who's on Top?

    Managers often ask me this question about sending carbon copies: "How should the list of names of those receiving copies appear at the bottom of a letter? Should they be listed alphabetically or by rank?" Here's the best guide:

(a) If you are sending copies to people of equal status, arrange the names alphabetically.

(b) If you are writing to people of widely differing ranks—especially if one person is very high up—you should defer to the top person by listing him or her first. Some organizations are so conservative that it's considered impolite to send a carbon copy to the very top brass: they expect their own freshly typed copy. Ask those in the know if this is the situation where you work.

GETTING ACTION FROM YOUR WRITING

It all seemed so simple. In your mind you knew clearly what you wanted to ask, you sat down at your terminal to put your thoughts on paper, and you mailed off your letter. Simple. Except, several weeks later you received a letter that seemed to be written in response to someone else. Maybe the problem was yours. Maybe you weren't as clear as you thought you had been.

    On the facing page is a sample of a letter written by an anxious consumer. His new purchase was defective, and he was trying to get it fixed under the provisions of a company warranty. If you were an employee of the Euripides Paper Shredder Company's customer relations section, wouldn't you have been confused?

    Don's letter has lots of problems. Even though it probably took him only five minutes to dash off, each follow-up letter that he writes to explain the previous one will take twice as long. He may end up making a costly call to Idaho.

    Here are several strategies to ensure a positive response from your letter and to save you from Don's dilemma.

- Make sure you state the subject of your letter in your reference headline after RE. If you feel it's not offensive, state the request here instead.

- Begin with your real purpose. Rarely are enclosures or attachments your most important point—so don't begin with them.

- Choose a tone appropriate to the situation. Avoid angry or insinuating remarks if you're writing a complaint. These will get you nowhere.

- Express your positive expectations for cooperation. A note of warmth always helps.

- Supply only enough background material to orient the reader to the situation. More than this might obscure your request.

Issues We All Face

```
The Euripides Paper Shredder Company
Consumer Relations
11540 Columbus Roadway
Melrose, ID 30957


Dear Customer Relations Supervisor:

I am enclosing one of the broken parts from my new desk-top
paper shredder, but the other part that broke (it had a
yellow extension with a red handle), was thrown out by my
secretary who got sick of staring at it while I was busy
looking for your warranty. The red handle was broken right
in two, believe me.

I really appreciate your guarantee to replace broken
parts. And I hope that you will make an allowance for my
secretary's having thrown out the other broken part
instead of understanding that we had to save it.


Thank you very much.

Sincerely,


Don T. Slippin
```

- Before you close, be sure your reader knows what to do. Request specific action: what, when, how.
- If the situation takes more than one page to explain, attach to your letter a memo with headlines that break down the problem and describe it in more detail. The last headline should read "Action Requested."

Check all of your important letters to see that they follow these getting-action strategies.

Now, pretend that you are Don T. Slippin and you just purchased the desk-top shredder only to find that two parts were broken. How would you notify the Euripides Paper Shredder Company of your misfortune so that you get your desired action—the replacement of the two defective parts? Write your letter on the following page.

How did you do? On page 94 is one way to write to the Euripides Paper Shredder Company. How does your letter compare?

Let's examine the contents of the first letter. Do you think the reader had these secret thoughts?

Letter Content	Reader Response
1. One broken part of the new desk-top paper shredder is enclosed.	*1. Unclear explanation*
2. Secretary threw out other part.	*2. Who cares who did it?*
3. I almost lost your warranty.	*3. A blunderer.*
4. I like your guarantee to replace broken parts.	*4. But do you want your new parts?*

Let's look at the likely reader response to the second letter.

Letter Content	Reader Response
1. I have a broken paper shredder made by your company.	*1. Aha, I see the problem stated.*
2. It came with two broken parts.	*2. Exact details.*
3. Only one part is enclosed.	*3. Parts described as clearly as possible.*
4. Your warranty promises to replace them.	*4. Positive expectations!*
5. Any problem, give me a call.	*5. Responsiveness/note of warmth.*
6. Please deliver two replacement parts.	*6. I see what you want.*

The letters speak for themselves.

ABSTRACT OBSCURITY

One day Ike Antwright was working on a memo describing market response to his company's recently developed personal computer, the SLXQ. He had discussed the trends, growth indicators and general market response. He wanted to explain why the sales were not so high as predicted using sentences such as this:

> The SLXQ has not met with the high degree of public acceptance predicted. Many customers seem to find the equipment too intimidating or cumbersome to learn to operate.

While this is useful information, it is very general and abstract. It needs to be followed with actual examples in order to come alive. To maintain reader interest and to clarify his point, Ike should follow the above statement with a real-life example—perhaps the story of Mr. Z, in Houston, who bought an SLXQ only to discover that it was too frustrating to operate.

The Euripides Paper Shredder Company
Consumer Relations Department
11540 Columbus Roadway
Melrose, ID 30957

RE: Defective Paper Shredder

Dear Customer Relations Supervisor:

Two days ago, I purchased a new desk-top paper shredder
manufactured by your company. Unfortunately, the shredder
had two broken parts. Since your company has such a fine
reputation, I am sure that you will replace the two
defective parts as soon as possible, as your warranty
promises.

Only one of the broken parts is enclosed. The other, a
yellow piece with a red handle attached, was accidentally
thrown away. Please accept my word that the second part was
broken when purchased.

If you have any further questions, please telephone me. If
not, I would appreciate your speedy action in delivering
the two replacement parts to me. The shredder was a gift to
my boss, and I promised to get a new one for her.

Thank you for your help with this.

Sincerely,

Don T. Slippin
127 Redwood Road
Altoona, R.I.
Tel. 722-337-9090

Anecdotes and examples illustrate your abstract ideas, making them come alive. Without examples your writing will seem dry or overly intellectual. Another problem with excessively abstract writing is that it can be easily misinterpreted. Consider this sentence:

The atmosphere in the conference room contributed to the outcome of the meeting.

Does it mean:

The hostility and backbiting among the committee members in the conference room contributed to the rejection of the proposal.

Or does it mean:

The supportive atmosphere in the conference room contributed to the exceptionally productive meeting.

Whenever possible, choose concrete words to express your ideas. Abstract writing is open to many interpretations, all potentially inaccurate. Therefore you must make a real effort to clarify your ideas and explain them so that the reader understands your intention. Give examples and add words that create a picture in the reader's mind. Words that relate to the senses—sight, sound, touch and smell —evoke the strongest response from readers.

Here are a few examples of abstract sentences followed by more concrete versions. Notice how much more helpful the second sentence is.

Abstract: The unit is malfunctioning.
Concrete: The TV doesn't work.
Abstract: He amassed major input to determine the functional requirements for console construction.
Concrete: He interviewed many experts to learn how to build the console.
Abstract: If a situation like this occurs in the future, please involve others in the office before taking action.
Concrete: If you ever find the office door unlocked again, please ask people about it before calling in the FBI.
Abstract: Due to extenuating circumstances, we will have to delay introduction of our new product line for a while.
Concrete: We've decided to delay introduction of our new product line for six months while we iron out a kink in the propulsion system.

How to lower the abstraction level in technical writing. The technical writers I meet spend a lot of time trying to explain unfamiliar information to their readers, yet they are the greatest sinners when it comes to being abstract. The best technical writers are the ones who reach out to the reader by offering real examples— examples they're sure readers can relate to.

When trying to explain an abstraction like aerodynamics, a good writer will risk cliché by referring to the wings of birds or the smooth, silver metal of a jet. Some writers in the technical world feel that giving examples and making creative comparisons is unprofessional. It's not. A real professional helps the reader however he can.

Abstract Obfuscation

Directions: The passage below is too abstract—it needs some concrete examples. Put an X between any sentences where an example would help:

> When writing a résumé you may find it hard to decide how much information to offer about your education. The more professional experience you have, the less you need to say about your training. Technical language should be kept to a minimum, since it can be inadvertently intimidating or confusing. Extracurricular activities and personal interests should not be given excessive attention on a résumé. Details of previous job experience should include a concise yet comprehensive description of responsibilities. Under the heading "Selected Accomplishments" you can list achievements that don't seem to fit in anywhere else.

Take a look at the same passage, this time with examples inserted. Aren't you surprised at how much difference the examples make?

> When writing a résumé you may find it hard to decide how much information to offer about your education. The more professional experience you have, the less you need to say about your training. For example, if you have worked in your profession for many years, you need not list courses taken in your college career. For an electrical engineer who is applying for a higher-paid job, a simple statement of his or her degrees and the names of schools attended suffices.
>
> Technical language should be kept to a minimum, since it can be inadvertently intimidating or confusing. A young chemist looking for a nonlaboratory job should not merely list courses with titles such as "Ionization of Crystalline Particles in Saline Solutions," which may give a misleading impression of primary career interests. He should also mention courses in marketing or management if they are relevant.
>
> Extracurricular activities and personal interests should not be given excessive attention on a résumé. Interviewers are unlikely to be overly impressed with a detailed account of an applicant's high school debate team's victories, summer hiking itineraries or musical preferences. A brief mention of major interests at the end of a résumé, under a heading such as "Activities and Interests" may, however, provide an employer with some helpful impressions of the individual and offer an opening for informal discussion during an interview.
>
> Details of previous job experience should include a concise yet comprehensive description of responsibilities. Clearly indicate dates of employment, titles, significant duties, number of staff supervised, scope of budget, special reports and projects completed and any promotions.
>
> Under the heading "Selected Accomplishments" you can list achievements that don't seem to fit in anywhere else. For example, you might mention awards,

volunteer work or special learning experiences. This category is especially helpful because it frees you from giving the traditional year-by-year account of your past.

Notice how the addition of examples enhanced your understanding of the original article. Suddenly it took on life and became far more helpful. Be watchful for places in your own writing where an example would reach out to your readers and add to their understanding.

MEASURING THE READABILITY LEVEL OF YOUR WRITING

Measuring readability means determining the reading level of a piece of writing. Can a sixth grader read and understand it? a tenth grader? a person with a graduate degree? This type of information is particularly useful for school textbook writers, who must be sure that they are communicating with young readers, but it also is important to any on-the-job writer.

At what level should you write? Asking this question is like asking, "How fast should you drive your car?" The answer, of course, depends on the situation. There is no one, correct, all-purpose reading level for all writing. You should always consider adjusting your writing level to meet the needs of your readers. You must ask, "Who are my readers?" Are they college graduates? highly skilled specialists? sales managers? computer scientists? vice-presidents? bookkeepers?

I measured the reading levels of a few publications myself. The results may surprise you.

New York *Times*—tenth-grade level
Reader's Digest—eighth-grade level
Winston Churchill's speeches—eighth-grade level
Wall Street Journal—thirteenth-grade level

Business Week—tenth-grade level
Gettysburg Address—tenth-grade level
People Magazine—eighth-grade level

Do these scores mean that you should write as if your readers were in high school? Not really. But tenth-grade is a good reading level to aim for if you're not sure who your reader is. Above that, you are running risks of being misunderstood. A tenth-grade level means avoiding too many long words and writing fairly short sentences. Focusing on vocabulary and the length of your sentences will help you adjust your writing level to your readers' ability.

In business, it is valuable to know how to write at different levels since, at various times, you may find yourself writing everything from a summary report for managers or a feasibility study for engineers to a set of procedures for clerical trainees.

Are you afraid you'll sound foolish if you lower your writing level? I am certainly *not* trying to suggest that you write in a juvenile way. It *is* possible to write a sophisticated and succinct sentence at the tenth-grade level.

To convince you that material of easy readability need not sound moronic, I enclose this quote from *On Writing Well,* by William Zinsser (New York: Harper & Row, 1976), a writing authority whose style we should all try to emulate. Its readability level: sixth grade.

> Style is organic to the person doing the writing, as much a part of him as his hair, or, if he is bald, his lack of it. Trying to add style is like adding a toupee. At first glance the formerly bald man looks young and even handsome. But at second glance—and with a toupee there is always a second glance—he doesn't look quite right. The problem is not that he doesn't look well groomed; he does, but we can only admire the wigmaker's almost perfect skill. The point is that he doesn't look like himself. [Page 19]

Here's another that rates a ninth-grade level.

> Who is this elusive creature the reader? He is a person with an attention span of about twenty seconds. He is assailed on every side by forces competing for his time: by newspapers and magazines, by television and radio and stereo, by his wife and children and pets, by his house and his yard and all the gadgets that he has bought to keep them spruce, and by that most potent of competitors, sleep. The man snoozing in his chair with an unfinished magazine open on his lap is a man who was being given too much unnecessary trouble by the writer.
>
> It won't do to say that the snoozing reader is too dumb or too lazy to keep pace with the train of thought. My sympathies are with him. If the reader is lost, it is generally because the writer has not been careful enough to keep him on the path. [Page 8]

The only way to judge if you are writing at the right reading level is to decide if the level is appropriate to your intended readers. Think about those readers—did you meet their needs?

To see how a readability score is derived, see Appendix B, "Fry's Readability Graph." It will help you understand what makes writing more or less readable.

The problem of technical writing. There are times when you cannot simplify the level of your writing, even if you want to. When you are writing on a technical subject, an abundance of technical vocabulary and numbers will necessarily make the text difficult to understand. If your readers are familiar with the subject matter, you probably shouldn't worry. But if you are trying to communicate technical information to nontechnical managers, stockholders or clients, be extremely careful to define or to translate terms they may be unfamiliar with. Pay special attention to shortening your sentences and try to use plenty of comparisons or concrete examples to help your reader.

If you suspect that your reader may lack interest or enthusiasm, make your writing as easy to read as possible. Again, the key to readability is short sentences and simple words.

HOW TO BE A DICTATOR

If you are fortunate enough to have access to dictating equipment, take advantage of it. You can record ideas six times faster by dictating than by writing, according to a study by the Department of Labor. While some executives pick up dictating skills instantly, few can dictate a perfect first draft. I meet many managers who say, "I keep losing my train of thought," or "I can't standing talking into a microphone." With practice and patience, dictation can be learned. And once you have mastered the Dictaphone, it does save time.

"I keep losing my train of thought." Consider the first complaint. Usually, the primary problem is the same, whether you dictate a first draft or write one—if you try to think of content and form at the same time you'll be in trouble. As we discussed in chapter 5, "Writing the First Draft," you must start by quickly writing your ideas without regard to sentence construction or word choice. The same goes for dictating. Accept the fact that you will have to edit the first, rough transcription. Warn whoever is doing your typing that this is not a final version. Perhaps giving the typist a little leeway—"It doesn't have to be perfectly typed this time"—will make retyping a few drafts seem less burdensome.

Before beginning to dictate, create a list-outline just as if you were starting a written memo. Use one of the five Start-Up Strategies to evolve your ideas. Choose the strategy that best suits your purpose and write down as many details as necessary to jog your memory as you dictate. Keep your list of ideas before you as you speak into the dictation equipment.

Don't let the machine get the best of you—when you need time to think, swallow or blow your nose, press the pause, or stop, button and relax. Replay the tape as often as necessary to check your transitions from one idea to the next. Speak slowly and clearly, indicating all punctuation marks and paragraph changes. And instruct your typist to transcribe the material with plenty of room for your editing: double-spaced, with very wide margins.

Remember, it is far easier to edit than to write. Once you are comfortable dictating a speedy, if imperfect, first draft, the time you save by doing so will allow you the leisure you need later for any revisions you may want to make.

"I can't stand talking into a microphone." What about the second complaint, the complaint of those who are uncomfortable talking to a machine? Most people with this problem are afraid of embarrassment. They dread sounding foolish or con-

fused. And their fear is not entirely unreasonable because almost every first draft sounds pretty lame—that is the nature of the beast. In order to learn to dictate you must be willing to risk sounding silly to start.

So what if your typist thinks you sound scatterbrained! Explain that you are dictating rough notes as a time-saving device. Get your typist's involvement and support for your dictating "experiment."

As with any of the six Start-Up Strategies, your goal is to put all your thoughts on paper before deciding which ones are valuable and which are useless. It is not necessary to be overly critical at the dictation stage. Your first draft, dictated or written, is your most creative moment. Try to suspend that judgmental inner voice long enough to let the ideas flow. If you can persevere through the self-conscious learning period, the dictating skills you acquire will more than justify your initial discomfort.

Dictating Hints

1. Prepare an outline or use a Start-Up Strategy to keep you on track.
2. At the beginning of the tape state the following:
   - Reader's name and address
   - Date of copy
   - Kind of writing—report, memo, letter
   - Type of paper
   - Approximate length
3. Signal when you don't want instructions or asides to appear in the actual copy. If something slips by you, don't worry. You'll be editing it before your reader sees it.
4. Indicate all punctuation marks, paragraph changes, and capitalizations. Spell out proper names and questionable words.
5. Write out directions to your typist for inserting any afterthoughts, quotes or footnotes.
6. Ask the typist to double-space for editing purposes.
7. Edit the typed copy yourself.

PART TWO

Quiz Yourself

The great artist
is the simplifier.
HENRI-FRÉDÉRIC AMIEL

8
What Are Your Personal Strengths and Weaknesses?

Now we turn to the critical editing skills you must apply after you've written your first draft. This part of the book consists of a series of miniquizzes to help you determine your strengths and weaknesses in the basic skills of writing: grammar, usage and punctuation. The rules I've presented are brief; my aim is to help you assess your skills quickly and to offer a short refresher. If you decide you need more explanation, instruction or practice, consult the books starred in the bibliography.

Each section begins with a pretest called "Quiz Yourself." Taking it will tell you if you need to complete that section. If you breeze through with a perfect score, go on to the next exercise. If you score below 100%, you'll be given a bit of instruction and more practice.

DANGLING MODIFIERS

Quiz Yourself
Decide whether each sentence is correct or incorrect. Check the appropriate box to the right of the sentence to indicate your answer.

	Correct	*Incorrect*
1. Sounding amazingly like a human voice, she played the flute every day after work.	☐	☐
2. Lifting the heavy metal desk all alone, a vein stood out in his neck.	☐	☐
3. Although he was only an assistant vice-president, the delivery boy brought him freshly brewed coffee twice a day.	☐	☐
4. As Director of Communications, several pioneering ideas became realities.	☐	☐

SCORING: 100%: Reward—go on to the quiz for gobbledygook. Less than 100%: Read the following rule and complete the practice exercise.

she was Director of Communications.
was only an assistant vice-president.   4. Incorrect: Several pioneering ideas became realities when
neck.   3. Incorrect: The delivery boy brought him freshly brewed coffee twice a day although he
human voice.   2. Incorrect: When he lifted the heavy metal desk all alone, a vein stood out in his
Answers: 1. Incorrect: Every day after work she played the flute, which sounded amazingly like a

RULE: Avoid dangling modifiers, phrases that do not logically or clearly modify a specific noun or pronoun. When you can't tell who or what the introductory word group refers to, add to or rearrange the sentence to include the proper information where needed. Hint: Pay special attention to the word directly after the comma. Does it belong there?

Example:

Packed in Styrofoam, you can ship the Fogg smoke detector anywhere.

Written this way, the sentence means that *you* are packed in Styrofoam, not the detector.

Here are two ways to correct this dangling modifier.

Solution #1: Add the missing subject (Fogg smoke detector) to the beginning of the main statement.

Packed in Styrofoam, the Fogg smoke detector can be shipped anywhere.

Solution #2: Add the subject (Fogg smoke detector) to the modifying phrase to make it a clause.

When the Fogg smoke detector is packed in Styrofoam, you can ship it anywhere.

Practice Exercise

Directions: Rewrite the sentences that contain dangling modifiers.* If the sentence is correct, mark it "Correct."

1. After spilling the soup at today's luncheon, the new Zappo contract was lost   _____
   by John.

2. While I was dictating the memo, the Dictaphone fell on my toe.   _____

3. Sitting in one chair for two solid hours, the secretary's foot fell asleep.   _____

4. By spreading the paint very thin, the painter can make one gallon cover the   _____
   entire office.

5. After dictating the letter, the mailman brought the mail which I read   _____
   quickly.

*See page 135 for corrected sentences.

6. When twelve years old, her uncle was promoted to vice-president of a multinational corporation. _____

7. Unless completely rewired, no engineers should handle the electrical equipment located in the rear basement. _____

8. Seeing a large gathering in the outer office, our curiosity was aroused. _____

9. While circling the airport, my mind was focused on the upcoming meeting. _____

10. Used for only two weeks, Jim expects to sell his home computer for slightly less than its original cost. _____

GOBBLEDYGOOK

Quiz Yourself

George Orwell said, "Never use a long word where a short one will do." Which of these sentences contain gobbledygook, A or B? Gobbledygook is stuffy, pompous language used for the sole purpose of trying to sound more professional.

	A	B
1. (A) The company must turn to top-priority tasks to reach its goal.	☐	☐
(B) It is now incumbent on the company to prioritize its tasks within the parameters of its goal expectation.		
2. (A) Andrea's real skill performance on the job showed a negative correlation with her potential skill performance.	☐	☐
(B) Andrea did not do as well in the job as she could have.		
3. (A) In answer to your letter of January 26, I am working on a solution that will be mutually satisfactory.	☐	☐
(B) Regarding your letter of January 26, which I am now in possession of, I beg your indulgence while I frame a response that does not give preferential treatment to either your company or ours.		
4. (A) At the agency, the work-difficulty element involved rendered inoperative their expectation of task completion within the originally prescribed time-frame.	☐	☐
(B) The agency's work was so difficult that the employees did not finish on time.		

SCORING: 100%: Reward—go on to the quiz for streamlining. Less than 100%: Read the rule and complete the practice exercise.

Answers: 1. B; 2. A; 3. B; 4. A

Gobbledygook can include jargon, the special vocabulary of a technical field that can mystify audiences unfamiliar with its meaning. Inflated words always cloud your message and are less than impressive to an educated reader. Using gobbledygook makes you sound stuffy, phony and insecure—something no manager can afford. Your straightforwardness will be appreciated.

RULE: To avoid gobbledygook, use the simplest, most concise language that will accurately express your ideas.

Example:

> We would like to ask that you endeavor to locate the communication for the reason that the manager deems it is of great import.

Better:

> Please try to find the letter because the manager feels it is very important.

Practice Exercise

Directions: Rewrite the following sentences to eliminate gobbledygook.*

1. Nevertheless, the termination of the product line will facilitate the advancement of the company's overall sales.

2. We would like to ask that you forward your spouse's Social Security number to the firm at your earliest convenience.

3. In view of the fact that the treasurer deems it important to institute a policy terminating managers over age sixty-eight, we will peruse his recommendations most seriously.

4. During the course of the week, Mr. Jones has utilized every available source to locate the materials.

5. We are in need of your assistance in ascertaining what has transpired since we first communicated.

6. Your cooperation in obtaining information as to the residences of employees hired prior to 1976 would be appreciated.

7. Did you obtain a copy of Mr. Quibble's communication requesting all personnel to indicate in writing when they intend to make use of a company vehicle?

8. I am contacting you with respect to initiating a stress management program within the confines of our office building.

9. Did you sustain any mental or physical injuries as a consequence of the accident?

10. We would like to request that you comply with the ensuing directions and complete the attached forms in detail.

*There are many correct solutions: see mine on page 135.

STREAMLINING

Quiz Yourself

Decide whether each sentence needs streamlining. Indicate your answer at the right.

	Yes	No
1. The critical factor here is to make sure that all the machines that are heavily used are checked not fewer than two times a year.	☐	☐
2. The information provided in this writing seminar can only make improvements in my future written assignments required for the job.	☐	☐
3. He has accomplished the development of many excellent computer programs for more than one company, which therefore seems to have given him the experience and knowledge of the skills necessary to succeed in this position.	☐	☐
4. Our requirement is to make available the ability to prepare several versions of expense units based on probable variations.	☐	☐

SCORING: 100%: Reward—go on to the quiz for the active voice. Less than 100%: Read the rule and complete the practice exercise.

Answers: 1. Yes: It is critical to check all heavily used machines at least twice a year. 2. Yes: This writing seminar can only improve my future on-the-job writing. 3. Yes: He has developed many excellent computer programs for companies, so he has the experience and skill to succeed in this position. 4. Yes: We must be able to prepare several versions of expense units based on probable variations.

Some sentences use too many words to express a simple thought. To prevent wordiness, ask yourself, "What is my message here?"

RULE: Streamlining means weeding out any words or phrases that do not contribute to the reader's understanding. Streamlining can also mean using a single word that summarizes a group of words; for example, "now" easily replaces "at this point in time."

Example #1:
You have asked the question as to what our fees would be.

Better:
You asked about our fees.

Example #2:
If the stock arrives without any identification as to whom it belongs to, it can involve quite a bit of time in tracking it down.

Better:
Tracking down stock that is not properly identified can be time-consuming.

Practice Exercise

Directions: Streamline the following sentences by omitting or changing unnecessary words or phrases, rearranging sections or dividing sentences.*

1. I certainly appreciated the chance to have the opportunity to meet with you and Arthur Forbes for lunch today, and I hope that you found the discussion to be worthwhile.

2. This letter is just a note to be sure that you and I understand what you said would be the criteria for determining the qualifications we are looking for in a new programmer for Section B.

3. What I have done is read every one of the invoices in question and pulled all the ones that I think we should have the bookkeeper look at.

4. I have a meeting scheduled with Mr. Blank on Monday to go over our fees and a few of the new requirements that some companies are asking me for.

5. Enclosed you will find various selected pages from the draft volume of the *Analysis Guide* which is being developed to help assist operators in the implementation of the new form of software.

6. As a result of a recent meeting I just had with the Personnel Department, I feel it is warranted that I recommend the hiring of Fred Blugh for the position of Security Guard, which he seems well qualified for.

7. The reason for the computer blowup yesterday is really that the error file has been increasing daily, and yesterday was the day that it went over one hundred items.

8. In the unusual event that we might want to make an adjustment to the totals for any reason on the following day, we can make the needed adjustment by manually altering the figures.

9. Although implementation of some of these recommendations would have an impact on the print shop as well, it was felt that the nature of this impact would be beneficial rather than adverse to the print shop operation.

10. Recently I have been receiving some complaints from some nonsmoking personnel whose most common complaint is that a nonsmoker accuses the person smoking of blowing the smoke in his direction.

11. Inasmuch as the same reason was always given for all three overdrafts, it seems that it might be due to a lack of internal communication in your bank.

*Streamlined sentences are on pages 135–36.

12. I am now in the process of duplicating my draft and plan on spending some time working tonight so that my secretary may have it retyped and delivered to you by noon tomorrow.

13. If there is any further information you need, please do not hesitate to contact me.

THE ACTIVE VOICE

Quiz Yourself
Which of these sentences are better, A or B?

	A	B

1. (A) Many important novels of American life were written by John Steinbeck.   ☐ ☐
   (B) John Steinbeck wrote many important novels of American life.

2. (A) The person on my right cleared the desk and the person on my left swept the floor.   ☐ ☐
   (B) The desk was cleared by the person on my right and the floor swept by the person on my left.

3. (A) You can give suggestions and comments about this memo without hurting my feelings.   ☐ ☐
   (B) Suggestions and comments can be given about this memo without hurting my feelings.

4. (A) The astronomy lecture was delivered to a large audience, and the speaker was animated and clear.   ☐ ☐
   (B) The speaker, who was animated and clear, delivered the astronomy lecture to a large audience.

SCORING: 100%: Reward—go on to the quiz for parallelism. Less than 100%: Read the rule and complete the practice exercise.

Answers: 1. B; 2. A; 3. A; 4. B

Business writers unconsciously overuse the passive voice in sentences like this one: "It is assumed the guidelines will be complied with." We are left to guess who is responsible for compliance—not to mention who assumes it. The active version is more straightforward and informative: "I assume that your company will comply with the guidelines."

Writing in the passive voice, as the word implies, makes you sound ineffectual. It shows an unwillingness to take responsibility for your actions. Remember Nixon's evasive statement, "The tapes were erased." Don't hide behind statements like "Your help is appreciated." Say "I (or we) appreciate your help." And so often we fail to give credit where it is due: "An excellent job was done." By whom?

Of course sometimes the passive is the best solution: "The contract was lost by bungling." Perhaps we'd rather not embarrass someone.

RULE: Use the active voice as often as possible.

Example:

Whenever possible, the passive voice should be avoided.

Better:

Whenever possible, avoid the passive voice.

Practice Exercise

Directions: Change the following sentences from the passive to the active voice by rearranging them so that you show who or what is the agent—the doer of the action.* Supply an agent if necessary.

1. Her proposal ought to be given our serious consideration.

2. A decision has to be reached soon or the contract may be lost.

3. An analysis of this toxic substance will be disclosed soon.

4. All the lights should be turned off before you leave the office.

5. It is expected that our president will be told that our best client was hopelessly alienated by our new salesperson.

6. Yesterday it was raining hard, so we were prevented from moving the equipment.

7. It has been decided that a time clock will be installed.

8. This conference, as was true also of the last one, was made possible through the outstanding organizing abilities of one person.

9. A good time was had by everyone.

10. This intolerable situation must be remedied immediately.

11. His excuse for being late was that he was delayed by a traffic jam.

12. He was advised by his supervisor to apply for the new position.

*See page 136 for corrected sentences.

PARALLELISM

Quiz Yourself
Decide whether these sentences are correct or incorrect.

	Correct	Incorrect
1. The damage was worse than they had anticipated: the rugs were stained, flood damage, and some wiring had to be replaced.	☐	☐
2. Her skills for the new job included researching, organization and writing of long reports.	☐	☐
3. His prospective employer required five references, but his résumé contained only four, so he was worried about his chances of obtaining the job.	☐	☐
4. The personnel department couldn't decide between rental and buying a third Xerox machine for the upcoming rush.	☐	☐

SCORING: 100%: Reward—go on to the quiz for consistency. Less than 100%: Read the rule and complete the practice exercise.

Answers: 1. Incorrect: flood damage was extensive 2. Incorrect: organizing 3. Correct 4. Incorrect: between renting and buying

RULE: In a sentence or a list, present parallel ideas in parallel form. In other words, sentence elements that function identically should be constructed identically. To achieve this harmony and equality of ideas, choose one form of a word, phrase or clause and stick to it. Parallel sentence elements channel the reader's attention.

Example:

His typing is fast and he does it accurately.

Solution:

His typing is fast and accurate.

Practice Exercise
Directions: In the following sentences, correct the errors in parallelism.* Mark "Correct" if the sentence is already correct.

1. The agenda for the meeting is as follows:
   a. calling the meeting to order   c. taking the roll call
   b. set date for next meeting   d. electing new officers
2. The safety committee voted:
   a. to install lighting in the parking areas
   b. to replace handrails on the stairway
   c. that faulty electrical outlets should be replaced
   d. to improve clearing ice from the walks

*See pages 136–37 for corrections.

3. We think she is imaginative, resourceful and thorough, and we recommend her for a job.

4. When you make the list, arrange the items in order of importance, write them in parallel form and all the items should be numbered.

5. She wrote a disorganized and incomplete report, and many words were misspelled, too.

6. He slept through his alarm, missed the bus and lost his wallet, all in the same day.

7. He is efficient, thorough and has a lot of imagination in his work.

8. By next Monday, please complete the survey, analyze the statistics, and you should hand in your report.

9. He enjoyed his new job for many reasons: the challenge, the salary, and it was a good working environment.

10. To conserve energy, follow this procedure when you leave the office:
    a. check that all electrical equipment has been turned off
    b. make sure all windows are closed
    c. are any lights left on?

CONSISTENCY

Quiz Yourself
Are the following sentences correct or incorrect? Indicate your answer on the right.

	Correct	Incorrect
1. Sometimes a person gives short shrift to exercise because they don't know how to fit it into a busy schedule.	☐	☐
2. It was the third time that she missed her bus and was late for work. Finally, she falls into her chair, exhausted before the day begins. How long could she go on this way?	☐	☐
3. The office needed a long table for conferences, but it also required a new filing cabinet and a place to store old correspondence.	☐	☐
4. Is it possible that television is a disruptive force in society? Do they keep us from reading books and magazines, traditionally the primary sources for obtaining information?	☐	☐

SCORING: 100%: Reward—go on to the quiz for logical comparisons. Less than 100%: Read the rule and complete the practice exercise.

Answers: 1. Incorrect: Sometimes a person/because he (or she) doesn't *or* Sometimes people/ because they don't 2. Incorrect: fell/ began 3. Correct 4. Incorrect: Does it keep us

RULE: Sentences and paragraphs should be consistent in tense, in agreement of verbs with subject and in use of pronouns. Proper relationships assure a logical progression of ideas. When words, phrases or clauses function the same way, construct them the same way. Continuity and symmetry are keys to good writing.

Examples: Here are three different types of inconsistency: tense, verb-subject and pronoun. A correct version follows each incorrect sentence.

Incorrect:

    Today the Director of Training, Mr. Hall, will appoint several new people to the committee. On his list were Kathy, Brad and Helen.

Correct:

    Today the Director of Training, Mr. Hall, will appoint several new people to the committee. On his list are Kathy, Brad and Helen.

Incorrect:

    Each of the day-shift employees go out to lunch.

Correct:

    Each of the day-shift employees goes out to lunch.

Incorrect:

    When one has a cold they should drink plenty of fluids.

Correct:

    When one has a cold one should drink plenty of fluids.

Practice Exercise

Directions: Find and underline the inconsistencies in the following examples. Write the correction(s) in the space provided.*

1. Sometimes a person cannot decide whether they would rather have a raise or a vacation.

2. The computer is a time-saving, space-saving invention. They are not difficult to use.

3. To change this typewriter ribbon, first turn off the machine. Open the lid and release the red lever. Do not try to lift out the ribbon cartridge until you release the lever. Once the lever was released, the cartridge comes off easily.

4. Arriving late at work is a problem we all have from time to time. Sometimes we are late because family responsibilities conflict with work responsibilities and you feel caught in the middle.

5. He ran up the steps, whirled through the revolving door and tangles his coat in the door.

*See page 137.

6. Routine tasks we can do almost without thinking. New tasks require greater concentration, but all tasks require attention to detail. Alternating the routine with the new provides a manner of refreshment and help ensure that our attention to detail never waivers.

7. The typewriter was developed during the nineteenth century. At first they had no shift-key mechanism and typed only in capital letters.

8. On the day before her vacation, she handed in her report, answered all pending correspondence and organizes her desk.

9. Concentration is the greater part of any skill. If a person wishes to learn a new skill, they must know how to concentrate.

10. If a reader wants to increase his reading speed, he should first learn to examine the entire book or article in question. He should learn to gather the big ideas in a selection before looking at the details. You should strive to master this technique in order to read more quickly.

MAKING LOGICAL COMPARISONS

Quiz Yourself

Decide whether the following sentences are correct or incorrect and check the appropriate boxes.

	Correct	Incorrect
1. The new employee's Spanish was better than many native speakers.	☐	☐
2. He was better prepared for his speech than any other speech I've heard in a long time.	☐	☐
3. The consultant's time-management study proved that our policy is more efficient than ITT.	☐	☐
4. My office is bigger than my boss.	☐	☐

SCORING: 100%: Reward—go on to the quiz for pronoun agreement. Less than 100%: Read the rule and complete the practice exercise.

Answers: 1. Incorrect: better than that of many 2. Incorrect: than any other speaker I've heard 3. Incorrect: than ITT's 4. Incorrect: than my boss's *or* than that of my boss

RULE #1: When making comparisons, make sure to identify clearly the parallels or differences between the things you compare. A logical comparison can only be made between things of the same class.

RULE #2: If you want to make two comparisons in the same sentence, be sure to complete the first before starting the second.

Practice Exercise

Directions: The following sentences are ambiguous as they stand. Delete, add or rearrange words as needed to make logical comparisons.*

1. Our policies are different from Lang Realty.

2. Boston Oil's policy on absenteeism is like Acme Industries.

3. This is one of the best, if not the best, product we manufacture.

4. I know the treasurer better than the general manager.

5. Jim's cash outlay amounted to fifty dollars more than his partner.

6. Rob plays golf more than his friends.

7. Our health benefits are different from our competitor.

8. Sarah's sales report is better organized than her assistant.

PRONOUN AGREEMENT

Quiz Yourself

Are these sentences correct or incorrect? Check the appropriate box for each.

	Correct	Incorrect
1. Susan was clearer than me about her choice for president.	☐	☐
2. Between you and I, I feel that the proposal was not fair to minority groups.	☐	☐
3. Us optimists have to stick together.	☐	☐
4. If a person makes a mistake, they should admit it, and not hide the truth.	☐	☐

SCORING: 100%: Reward—go on to the quiz for commas. Less than 100%: Read the rule and complete the practice exercise.

Answers: 1. Incorrect: clearer than I 2. Incorrect: Between you and me 3. Incorrect: We optimists 4. Incorrect: he or she should admit it

RULE #1: If a pronoun replaces the subject of a clause or sentence, use:

Singular	Plural
I	we
you	you
he	they
she	
it	

*See page 137 for corrections.

Example #1:

The devil made me do it.   He made me do it.

RULE #2: If a pronoun replaces the object of a verb or preposition, use:

Singular	*Plural*
me	us
you	you
him	them
her	
it	

Example #2:

The memo praised Brian.   The memo praised him.

Remember: Before choosing a pronoun, determine how you will use it in the sentence.

Practice Exercise

Directions: Think carefully about the function of each pronoun in the sentences below. Circle the correct form.*

Example:

Are you going to leave with ((them,) they) or (we,(us))?

1. Between you and (I, me), the company seems on the edge of bankruptcy.
2. Two men, Dale and (he, him), made the decision.
3. (We, Us) architects must consider beauty as well as strength in our designs.
4. Mr. Skeffington showed (we, us) newcomers the training film.
5. Hal was more irritated about the bill than (I, me).
6. (She, Her) and (me, I) were the only ones who could have done the job.
7. James has always been more organized than (her, she).
8. Among (us, we) executives at the conference, there were many from Chicago.
9. Alice and (she, her) wrote the speech.
10. The award for the best speech of the year went to Alice and (she, her).

USING COMMAS AROUND PHRASES

Quiz Yourself

Which sentences require commas? Circle the number before each sentence that needs a comma and indicate where the commas should go.

1. Steven Marx who has a melodious voice is very effective on the telephone.
2. The office that he works in is spacious.

*Answers are on page 137.

3. Anyone who has studied computer programing has an edge in today's job market.

4. He will take advice from any person he considers knowledgeable.

5. This system which has been tested in twenty-five major office buildings across the country is infallible.

SCORING: 100%: Reward—go on to the quiz for semicolons. Less than 100%: Read the rule and complete the practice exercise.

RULE: Use commas around phrases when the information in the clause offers added facts about the subject.

If the phrase could be put in parentheses or dropped out of the sentence, use commas to set it off.

Example #1:

Mr. Thompson, who is in his late fifties, is the owner of the firm.

Solution #1: The clause "who is in his late fifties" is an added fact about Mr. Thompson. You could put it in parentheses and not alter the meaning of the sentence. Therefore, use commas.

Example #2:

All employees who work this Sunday will be paid overtime.

Solution #2: The clause "who work this Sunday" could not be put in parentheses. It alters the meaning of the sentence by answering the question "which employees?" Therefore, do not use commas.

Practice Exercise

Directions: Supply the missing commas where needed.*

1. Our company which employs 1,800 people is the largest manufacturer in the area.

2. The men and women who work in management are well motivated.

3. People will usually try harder for a boss whom they consider fair.

4. The earth which has a limited amount of fossil fuel resources can only support a finite number of people and their homes, cars, planes and offices.

5. Any person who is as intelligent as Donna can have a job with the firm.

6. I have never known a manager who was as efficient as Frank.

7. Janet Brock who has never missed a day of work was promoted yesterday.

8. I believe that a firm should not manufacture any product that is useless to society.

9. This desk which was purchased in 1952 is Mr. Dooley's pride and joy.

10. Often the people who are the loudest have the least to say.

*See page 138.

SEMICOLONS

Quiz Yourself
Are these sentences correct or incorrect?

	Correct	Incorrect

1. The department's trip to the Ice Follies was canceled; because of the bad storm and the warning of local authorities to stay off the roads. ☐ ☐
2. The dog is an orphan, we found him abandoned in a cardboard box. ☐ ☐
3. Our two new word processors take up a lot of office space, consequently, we must now rearrange the furniture. ☐ ☐
4. Working in the training department was a wise choice for Nancy; she is a natural with people. ☐ ☐

SCORING: 100%: Reward—go on to the quiz for colons. Less than 100%: Read the rule and complete the practice exercise.

Answers: 1. Incorrect (no semicolon) 2. Incorrect: orphan; we found 3. Incorrect: space; conse- quently, 4. Correct

RULE #1: Use a semicolon to link two complete sentences.
Example #1:
> We cannot predict how long the study will take; we have never conducted this kind of study before.

RULE #2: Use a semicolon to precede clauses that begin with adverbs such as "however," "moreover," "therefore," "consequently" or "for example."
Example #2:
> This training manual is confusing; moreover, it lacks an index and a table of contents.

RULE #3: Use a semicolon to separate a list or series when it already has commas in it.
Example #3:
> The three people authorized to sign the check are Mr. Davis, the president; Ms. Shelby, the treasurer; and Mr. Trawler, the office manager.

Practice Exercise
Directions: Decide which sentences below require semicolons. Write the correct punctuation and the word preceding it on the line provided.*

1. This is the warmest corner of the office it gets direct afternoon sun. _____
2. The department needs the new equipment however, there is no room to install it. _____
3. Everyone will contribute something to the staff party for example, cheese, crackers, cider, soda, cake or cookies. _____

*See page 138 for correct answers.

4. When I'm on time, no one notices when I'm late the whole office _____ knows.

5. The telephone survey indicated that the bank's services were little- _____ known consequently the PR Department instituted a new publicity campaign.

6. The managers had planned to discontinue that service however, an _____ overwhelming customer demand persuaded them to retain it.

7. We enjoyed and learned from our visit to the word-processing _____ department moreover, we were glad to meet the staff.

8. We are tightening security therefore we will not issue night passes _____ this year.

9. This problem appears to be serious we should hire a consultant. _____

10. We have several choices all of them are interesting. _____

11. She dislikes committee work consequently, she declined the posi- _____ tion.

12. One was promoted the other two quit. _____

13. If you need more exercise, don't use the elevator take the stairs. _____

14. We would like to give him a farewell party however, he would _____ prefer that we do not.

15. We cannot meet this deadline we would like an extension. _____

16. He opened my mail for me while I was on vacation he even _____ answered most of my letters.

17. The job carries several diverse responsibilities for example, prepar- _____ ing the budget, designing and implementing new systems and overseeing a staff of six.

18. We have several choices, all of them interesting. _____

19. The company softball team lost two out of three games this sum- _____ mer, but morale remained high.

COLONS

Quiz Yourself

Which of these sentences are punctuated correctly?

	Correct	Incorrect
1. Marianne is brilliant in her field: artificial intelligence.	☐	☐
2. We need to order the following; 500 letterheads, 500 envelopes, 1,000 sticky labels and 3 reams of typing paper.	☐	☐
3. Whoever enters the room next gets this envelope: it's the door prize.	☐	☐
4. Dear Ms. Merton,	☐	☐

SCORING: 100%: Reward—go on to the quiz for dashes. Less than 100%: Read the rule and complete the practice exercise.

RULE #1: Use a colon after a surname in the salutation of a business letter.
Example #1:

Dear Ms. Culpepper:

RULE #2: Use a colon to link a list or series to its connecting thought.
Example #2:

Six states are participating in the conference: New Jersey, Oklahoma, New York, Florida, Texas and California.

RULE #3: Use a colon to introduce an amplification of a statement or idea. When used this way the colon replaces such words as "that is" or "namely."
Example #3:

There is only one way to do things: the right way.

Practice Exercise

Directions: Decide where colons should replace commas.* Write the new punctuation and word preceding it in the space provided. Mark "Correct" if the sentence is correct as is.

1. Make an outline, headline each paragraph, begin each paragraph with a topic sentence, and proofread for spelling and punctuation. _____

2. Several of the smaller, more common office supplies were automated within the last few years, the pencil sharpener, the eraser, the stapler, the paper punch. _____

3. The nurse gave him the same old advice, drink plenty of liquids, get lots of rest, and eat oranges. _____

4. We have three salesmen in each district, the Northeast, the mid-Atlantic states, the Northwest, the Southwest. _____

5. The board met in January but could not take a vote, the chairwoman, the secretary, the treasurer and two members were absent with the flu. _____

6. There is only one thing to dispel the midwinter gloom in this office, a party. _____

7. Vacation time increases with length of service, one week the first year, two weeks the second through the fifth year, three weeks thereafter. _____

8. We cannot begin without the following supplies, 500 envelopes, a ream of paper, 500 mailing labels, elastic bands. _____

9. We all know why business is booming, Christmas is a week away. _____

10. Dear Fred, _____

*See page 138 for answers.

Quiz Yourself

DASHES

Which of these sentences are punctuated correctly?

	Correct	Incorrect

1. Four designers received top honors in the competition—but no one was there to accept the prizes. ☐ ☐
2. The book begins with the simplest writing task—a short letter or memo —and then moves on to more challenging issues. ☐ ☐
3. Please wait—while I run back for my pocketbook. ☐ ☐
4. Her eyes kept returning to the page—the blank page. ☐ ☐

SCORING: 100%: Reward—go on to the quiz for apostrophes. Less than 100%: Read the rule and complete the practice exercise.

Answers: 1. Correct 2. Correct 3. Incorrect (no dash) 4. Correct

RULE #1: Use a dash to indicate an emphatic pause.

Example #1:

He knew he was in trouble—the steam gauge had exploded.

RULE #2: Use a dash to repeat an idea for emphasis.

Example #2:

The office was cold—ice-cold.

RULE #3: Use dashes to set off an explanatory expression that needs emphasis.

Example #3

Herb brought the whole family—even the baby—to the office party.

Practice Exercise

Directions: Decide where a dash could be used to improve the following sentences. Write the new punctuation and the word(s) preceding and following it in the space provided.* Mark "Correct" if the sentence is already correct; some are correct either way.

1. The suburban branch will be closed by the end of this month, _____ unless its sales pick up unexpectedly.
2. He designed, produced, and distributed the posters you saw _____ around the building.
3. Only one computer, the XR70, can perform all the functions listed _____ here.
4. The manager was new to the firm, brand-new. _____
5. If I were you, and I'm glad I'm not, I'd rewrite the report. _____

*See answers on page 138.

6. All our employees, clerks included, are eligible for the profit-sharing plan after two years' consecutive service. _____

7. I gave many specific examples, all well documented. Still, no one understood the problem. _____

8. Please stop, I've heard all these arguments before. _____

9. If this trend continues, and there is no reason why it should not, we will show unprecedented profits this year. _____

10. You are the last one included in our retirement plan; you signed up just in time. _____

APOSTROPHES

Quiz Yourself

Which of these sentences are correct?

	Correct	Incorrect
1. When the package arrived in the mailroom, we were mystified by it's contents.	☐	☐
2. Look what she has accomplished in only two years time.	☐	☐
3. Genes happiness with the job was a pleasure to see, and his enthusiasm was contagious.	☐	☐
4. Please go to the back door; its the only one open.	☐	☐

SCORING: 100%: Enjoy reading the remainder of the book! Less than 100%: Read the rule and complete the practice exercise.

Answers: 1. Incorrect: its 2. Incorrect: years' 3. Incorrect: Gene's 4. Incorrect: it's

Most commonly, errors with apostrophes occur in connection with the possessive case and its relationship to plurals. These rules will help:

RULE #1: Form the possessive of a singular noun or a plural noun not ending in "s" by adding an apostrophe and an "s"; form the possessive of a plural noun ending in "s" by adding only the apostrophe. E.g., "the boss's desk," "the women's accomplishments," "the two technicians' findings."

RULE #2: Use the apostrophe alone, too, to form the possessive of plurals ending in "es," as in "the Joneses' house."

RULE #3: Apostrophes are traditionally used in forming the plural of letters and numbers or words referred to as words ("p's and q's"), but the more modern approach is to drop apostrophes whenever the meaning will not be affected—e.g., "1930s" or "Xenon 3900s." Always add both an apostrophe and an "s" to form the singular possessive, however ("the YMHA's building fund").

Practice Exercise

Directions: The following sentences are missing apostrophes. Put the nineteen missing apostrophes in their proper places.*

1. His glasses always seem to end up on Franks desk.
2. Fridays sales meeting was canceled on account of Mr. Jones illness.
3. The new assistants job is to proofread all of the defending lawyers and the prosecuting attorneys briefs before the trials.
4. Smith & Dawsons computer is the same model as Royal Regions.
5. Jims insistence that he can't work with Mary makes the offices atmosphere tense.
6. Working womens needs are different from working mens.
7. Sudden starts and stops wear down the machines gears and sprockets.
8. The mans office is across from the womens locker room.
9. She thought Sarahs reports were more carefully researched than either Dawns or hers.
10. The XR70s cost is greater than the 3200s, which was developed in the 1980s.

YOUR PERSONAL PROFILE

Now that you've polished your writing skills, you must start applying what you've learned to your daily writing. Editing your writing will be easier if you have a list of your strengths and weaknesses before you. This will remind you to apply actively what you've learned. Use the graph on page 124 to map your skills. Then make a list of your weaknesses and post it by your desk for quick reference when editing your writing.

How to fill out the graph: Flip back through the practice exercises in part two and note your strengths and weaknesses in each by calculating your percentage of correct answers. You should consider a score of less than 70% as a weakness.

To complete the profile, plot your scores on the graph shown on page 124. You might want to keep a copy of the graph next to the list by your desk to remind you of your strengths, too.

*See page 138.

PERSONAL PROFILE GRAPH

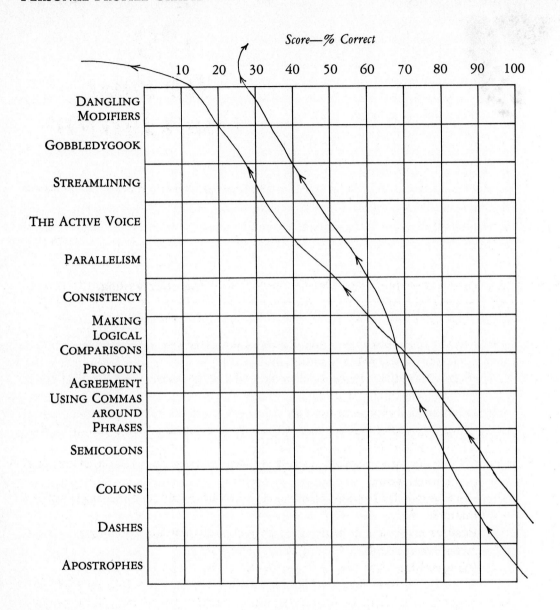

9
Be Your Own Editor

Now that you've put so much effort into improving your writing, it's time to become your own editor. Take something you've written recently and check it against the list below. Use this checklist for editing all of your future writing.

- Impact: Did you state "the bottom line" at the very beginning of your correspondence when appropriate?
- Ideas: Do your main ideas come first whenever possible, followed by those that are less important?
- Headlines: Did you use enough?
- Clear expectations: Did you make a clear request for action if you needed it?
- Completeness: Did you say everything you intended?
- Clarity: Did you employ modern language, rather than jargon, affectations or gobbledygook?
- Conciseness: Did you avoid using extra words or adding unnecessary subject matter?
- Positive approach: Is your correspondence upbeat and confident?
- Active voice: Did you avoid the passive voice?
- Paragraphing: Are your paragraphs short, with one idea in each?
- Sentence variety: Are your sentences varied in structure and length?
- Proofreading: Did you reread carefully to correct grammar, spelling, punctuation and facts?
- Readability level: Is it too high or too low? Does it suit your audience?
- Consistency: Is your point of view clear throughout?

On page 126 is a sample page of this book in the editing stage. If your revisions don't look like this at least once in the editing process, you're either a genius or a lazy editor.

> ~~Now~~ let's consider what would have happened if Hope had entered the meeting room without having put her proposal ~~on to~~ [on] paper. Imagine the reaction of senior, ~~or older~~ managers to the newcomer, Hope Striver, if she had opened ~~up~~ the meeting with words like these: "I'm here to tell you of my new promotion ~~scheme~~ [management plan]."

¶ ~~Paranoia would~~ [Cold, icy suspicion might] have ~~run rampant throughout~~ [filled] the room. ~~There would have been~~ No report or agenda [would have been available] for participants to scan. ~~In all likelihood, people would not initially have thought of the benefits of such a promotion initiative~~ [change to] Their first thoughts would probably have centered on their own job security ~~concerns~~. Without knowing that Hope had some weighty "persuaders" in mind, ~~she~~ [they] could easily have ~~been undercut at the finish of every sentence~~ [started raising objections after five minutes] if she had gotten that far in her presentation. The meeting could easily have turned into Hope's "baptism by fire" as a new employee at Polytrix.

And you can guess how the meeting would have ended. Some cool-headed, experienced manager would have ~~si- lenced the room with~~ [made] the suggestion that Hope go back to the drawing board and prepare a written report for consideration at a later date. Much later.

> It's not likely that the benefits of Hope's initiative would have occurred to most of those in attendance.

Proofreading. The importance of proofreading can never be stressed enough. One frequent problem is that no one knows whose responsibility it should be. The typist will say the letter's *writer* should do it; the writer will say it's the typist's job. In truth, if your name is signed at the bottom of a letter, *you* are responsible for correcting every misspelling, typo or punctuation error—in short, every detail.

Each piece of writing that leaves your office reflects your intelligence, thoroughness and effectiveness. You are sending an image of yourself into the world to be judged. Always take the extra few minutes to proofread your work; being too busy is no excuse. You'll find that the more polished and neat your correspondence is, the more respect you'll gain. Save yourself needless embarrassment—appear as successful as you are!

THE SPELLING CHEAT SHEET

If you're a bad speller, you probably hate using the dictionary, too. Who has the time? This spelling cheat sheet contains some of the most commonly misspelled words in business. Photocopy it or cut it out and keep it under your blotter. Use a yellow marker to highlight the words that are your particular problems.

An audit of your spelling ability would prove something interesting; each of us has a personal list of hard-to-spell words that are our special bugaboos. If you're stuck for a word that's not on the Cheat Sheet, find it in the dictionary and add it to the sheet. In other words, pinpoint your bugaboos once and for all so that next time they'll be just a glance away.

abbreviate	adjustment	analysis	associate
abruptly	admirable	analyze	assured
absence	advantageous	announce	attendance
absolutely	advertisement	announcement	attorneys
accede	advertising	annoyance	authorize
acceleration	advice	annual	available
accept	advisable	anticipate	
acceptance	advise	apologize	bankruptcy
accessible	adviser	apparent	bargain
accessory	advisory	appearance	basis
accidentally	affect	applicable	believable
accommodate	affidavit	applicant	believe
accompanying	aggravate	appointment	beneficial
accordance	agreeable	appraisal	beneficiary
accrued	allotment	appreciable	benefited
accumulate	allotted	appropriate	biennially
accuracy	allowable	approximate	bookkeeper
achievement	allowance	architect	brilliant
acknowledgment	all right	argument	brochure
acquaintance	almost	arrangement	budget
acquiesce	already	article	bulletin
acquire	although	ascertain	bureau
address	altogether	assessment	business
adequate	ambitious	assignment	calendar
adjourn	amendment	assistance	canceled

cancellation
candidate
capital
capitol
casualty
catalog
cease
ceiling
choice
choose
circumstances
client
clientele
collateral
column
commission
commitment
committee
comparable
compelled
competent
competitor
complement
compliment
compromise
concede
conceivable
conceive
concession
concurred
conference
confident
confidential
congratulate
conscience
conscientious
conscious
consensus
consequence
consignment
consistent
conspicuous

continual
continuous
controlling
controversy
convenience
convenient
cordially
correspondence
council
counsel
courteous
courtesy
creditor
criticism
criticize
current
customer

debtor
deceive
decision
deductible
defendant
defense
deferred
deficit
definite
definitely
delegate
dependent
depositors
describe
desirable
deteriorate
develop
development
device
devise
differed
difference
director
disappear

disappoint
discrepancy
dissatisfied
division
dual

eagerly
economical
effect
efficiency
efficient
either
eligible
eliminate
eminent
emphasis
emphasize
employee
endeavor
endorsement
enterprise
enthusiasm
envelop
envelope
environment
equipment
equipped
equivalent
especially
essential
etiquette
evident
exaggerate
exceed
excellence
excellent
except
excessive
exclusively
exercise
existence
expedite

expenditure
expense
experience
explanation
extension
extraordinary

facilities
familiarize
fascinate
favorable
favorite
feasible
February
financial
forcible
foreign
foreword
forfeit
formerly
forty
forward
fourth
freight
friend
fulfillment
furthermore

gauge
genuine
governor
grateful
grievance
guarantee

handled
harass
hardware
hazardous
height
hesitant
hindrance

identical
illegible
immediately
imminent
imperative
implement
inasmuch as
incidentally
inconvenience
incurred
indebtedness
independent
indispensable
individual
inducement
inference
inferred
influential
inquiry
installment
intelligence
intention
intercede
intercession
interfere
interrupted
inventory
investor
irregular
irrelevant
itemized
itinerary
it's, its

jeopardize
judgment
justifiable

knowledge

laboratory
legible

legitimate
leisure
letterhead
liaison
library
license
likable
likelihood
livelihood
loose
lose
luncheon

magazine
maintenance
management
manufacturer
manuscript
maximum
memorandum
merchandise
mileage
millennium
minimum
minuscule
mischievous
miscellaneous
modernize
mortgage

necessary
negligible
negotiate
neighborhood
neither
nevertheless
ninety
noticeable
nuisance

oblige
occasion

occupant
occurred
occurrence
occurring
offense
offering
official
omission
opportunity
optional
ordinary
organization
organize
original
overdue

pamphlet
parallel
partial
participant
particularly
patronage
perceive
percent
performance
permanent
permissible
permitted
perseverance
personal
personnel
persuade
planning
pleasant
pleasure
practical
practically
practice
precede
precision
preferable
preference

preferred
prejudice
preliminary
premium
previous
principal
principle
privilege
procedure
proceed
professor
prominent
prosecute
psychology
purchase
pursue

quantity
questionnaire
quiet
quite

realize
reasonable
receipt
receive
recently
recognize
recommend
recurrence
reference
referred
referring
regrettable
reimburse
remittance
renewal
repetition
representative
requirement
respectfully
respectively

responsibility
responsible
restaurant
ridiculous
route

salable
salary
satisfactorily
satisfying
schedule
secretary
securities
seized
separate
serviceable
several
severely
shipment
siege
significant

similar
simultaneous
sincerity
somewhat
specialize
specialty
stationary
stationery
statistics
strictly
submitted
subscriber
substantial
succeed
successful
sufficient
superintendent
supersede
supervisor
supposedly
survey

tariff
temporary
their
there
thorough
throughout
tragedy
transferred
typing

ultimately
unanimous
undoubtedly
unfortunately
unnecessary
unusually
until
usually

vacillate
vacuum

valuable
various
vehicle
vendor
vicinity
visible
voluntary
volunteer

warehouse
weather
weird
whether
wholly
withhold
worthwhile
writing

yield

APPENDIXES
SUGGESTED READING

APPENDIX A
Solutions to Exercises

THE ORGANIZATION GAME

   I.   Title Page   *P*
  II.   Table of Contents   *M*
 III.   Management Overview (Abstract)   *L*
 IV.   Recommendations for Purchase of Penny Counters   *F*
       A. Predicted Productivity Improvements   *N*
       B. Economic Advantages   *0*
   V.   Equipment Analysis   *D*
       A. Equipment Cost Justification   *C*
       B. Equipment Depreciation   *E*
       C. Vendor and Equipment Selection   *G*
 VI.   Implementation Considerations   *B*
       A. Implementation Timetable   *J*
       B. Implementation Plan   *H*
 VII.   Staffing Requirements   *A*
VIII.   Background   *I*
 IX.   Final Summary   *K*

PARAGRAPHS

In 1980, the United States faced what was believed to be an acute shortage of lunar rock analysis engineers that was predicted to get worse over the next decade. The 1981 Technology Training Act authorized substantial federal funds to increase the training of these high-technology professionals.

Universe University was one of fifteen space-shot engineering schools to compress its four-year curriculum into three years in order to train more astroengineers in a shorter time. Class size quickly jumped from 135 to 190 to meet special federal funding requirements.

The capacity to respond to changing professional and societal needs is incumbent upon leading institutions such as Universe University. In 1925, Universe University's Engineering School was one of the first in the nation to adopt the five-year curriculum so that new courses, and a more intensive presentation of old ones, could be provided.

Now that the lunar rock analysis engineering manpower crisis has passed, schools across the country are returning to pre-1980 curricula. Universe University has readopted its previous four-year format. All aspects of the school's educational and extracurricular programing will be back to normal until our next successful space probe.

IS YOUR WRITING TOO FORMAL?

1. to expect
2. to seem
3. to find out
4. to help
5. to work with
6. to think
7. to want
8. to figure, find
9. to show
10. to make
11. to try
12. to follow
13. to sign (as in a contract)
14. to send
15. to give
16. since
17. to say, show
18. first
19. instead of
20. if
21. to find
22. about
23. people
24. of, about
25. soon, now
26. before
27. to forbid
28. to ask for
29. to need
30. home, address
31. to show
32. to check
33. wife, husband
34. to say
35. enough
36. to send, give
37. to end, stop or fire
38. to happen

MARKETING LETTERS RESPONSE SHEET

1. The second one.
2. Pompous, insulting, condescending, cold.
3. Friendly, warm, sincere, down-to-earth.
4. Her own company.
5. The interests and needs of the potential client, Dewitt.
6. #2. It was lively and competent. Goodman sounded like a go-getter.
7. #2. She suggests an exact date. Good idea!

THE POSITIVE APPROACH

1. We're sure you will be pleased with the results.
2. With proper planning we can provide space for everyone.
3. As soon as you have paid the balance of your account we will gladly process your order.
4. Now, that's a baby!
5. We expect the changes to be beneficial.
6. Access to this information is essential.
7. If all goes well we will know we made the right decision.
8. The results of his research made a significant contribution to our final decision.
9. Pay attention to details; they are important.
10. This job is going to be challenging.

DANGLING MODIFIERS

1. After spilling the soup at today's luncheon, John lost the new Zappo contract.
2. Correct
3. The secretary's foot fell asleep after she sat in one chair for two solid hours.
4. Correct
5. After I dictated the letter, the mailman brought the mail. I read it quickly.
6. Her uncle was promoted to vice-president of a multinational corporation when she was twelve years old.
7. No engineers should handle the electrical equipment located in the rear basement unless the equipment is completely rewired.
8. Our curiosity was aroused after we saw a large gathering in the outer office.
9. While we circled the airport, my mind was focused on the upcoming meeting.
10. Jim expects to sell his home computer, used for only two weeks, for slightly less than its original cost.

GOBBLEDYGOOK

1. But dropping this product line will improve the company's overall sales.
2. Please send the firm your spouse's Social Security number as soon as possible.
3. Because the treasurer feels it is important to start letting go managers over age sixty-eight, we will read his recommendation seriously.
4. This week, Mr. Jones asked everybody he knew to help him find the materials.
5. We need your help in order to find out what happened since we first telephoned you.
6. Would you please help us find the home addresses of employees hired before 1976?
7. Did you get a copy of Mr. Quibble's memo asking all employees to inform him in writing when they need a company car?
8. Would you be interested in starting a stress management program in our office building?
9. Were you injured in the accident?
10. Kindly follow the directions and complete the attached forms in detail.

STREAMLINING

There are many correct solutions to these. Here are mine:

1. I was pleased to have lunch with you and Arthur Forbes today and hope you found our discussion worthwhile.
2. I want to confirm our criteria for determining the qualifications of a new Section B programmer.
3. I have pulled out the invoices I feel the bookkeeper should review.
4. On Monday, Mr. Blank and I will meet to discuss our fees and some new company requirements.
5. Enclosed are some pages from the draft of the *Analysis Guide* being developed to help operators implement the new software.

6. After meeting with the Personnel Department, I recommend Fred Blugh for the Security Guard position—he is well qualified.
7. The computer blew up yesterday because the error file went over one hundred items.
8. If we want to adjust the totals on the following day, we can do so manually.
9. Although these recommendations would affect the print shop, they would be beneficial.
10. Recently, nonsmokers have complained that smokers are blowing smoke in their direction.
11. Since the same reason was given for all three overdrafts, there may be a lack of internal communication in your bank.
12. I'll work on my draft tonight so that you'll have it tomorrow.
13. If you need more information, please contact me.

THE ACTIVE VOICE

1. We ought to give her proposal serious consideration.
2. We have to reach a decision soon or we may lose the contract.
3. Soon we will disclose an analysis of this toxic substance.
4. Turn off all the lights before you leave the office.
5. I expect someone to tell the president that our new salesperson hopelessly alienated our best client.
6. Yesterday the rain prevented us from moving the equipment.
7. He decided to install a time clock.
   or We have decided to install a time clock.
8. One person's outstanding organizing abilities made both this conference and the last one possible.
9. Everyone had a good time.
10. You must remedy this intolerable situation immediately.
11. His excuse for being late was that a traffic jam delayed him.
12. His supervisor advised him to apply for the new position.

PARALLELISM

There are two possible solutions to #1.   *Or:*

1. a. Correct   a. call the meeting to order
   b. setting the date for the next meeting   b. set the date for the next meeting
   c. Correct   c. take the roll call
   d. Correct   d. elect new officers
2. a. Correct
   b. Correct
   c. to replace faulty electrical outlets
   d. Correct
3. Correct
4. When you make the list, arrange the items in order of importance, write them in parallel form and number all the items.

5. She wrote a disorganized and incomplete report and misspelled many words.
6. Correct
7. He is efficient, thorough and very imaginative in his work.
8. By next Monday, please complete the survey, analyze the statistics and hand in your report.
9. He enjoyed his new job for many reasons: the challenge, the salary and the good working environment.
10. a. Correct
    b. Correct
    c. make sure no lights are left on *or* make sure all lights are turned off

CONSISTENCY

1. Sometimes people cannot decide whether they would rather have a raise or a vacation. *or* Sometimes a person cannot decide whether he (*or* she) would rather have a raise or a vacation.
2. It is not difficult to use.
3. Once you release the lever, the cartridge comes off easily.
4. Sometimes we are late because family responsibilities conflict with work responsibilities and we feel caught in the middle.
5. He ran up the steps, whirled through the revolving door and tangled his coat in the door.
6. Alternating the routine with the new provides a manner of refreshment and helps ensure that our attention to detail never waivers.
7. At first it had no shift-key mechanism and typed only in capital letters.
8. On the day before her vacation, she handed in her report, answered all pending correspondence and organized her desk.
9. If a person wishes to learn a new skill, he (*or* she) must know how to concentrate.
10. He should strive to master this technique in order to read more quickly.

MAKING LOGICAL COMPARISONS

1. Our policies are different from Lang Realty's (policies).
2. Boston Oil's policy on absenteeism is like Acme Industries' (policy).
3. This is one of the best products we manufacture, if not the best.
4. I know the treasurer better than I know the general manager.
5. Jim's cash outlay amounted to fifty dollars more than his partner's (cash outlay).
6. Rob plays golf more than his friends do.
7. Our health benefits are different from our competitor's (health benefits).
8. Sarah's sales report is better organized than her assistant's.

PRONOUN AGREEMENT

1. me 2. he 3. We 4. us 5. I 6. She, I 7. she 8. us 9. she 10. her

USING COMMAS AROUND PHRASES

1. Our company, which employs 1,800 people, is the largest manufacturer in the area.
2. Correct
3. Correct
4. The earth, which has a limited amount of fossil fuel resources, can only support a finite number of people and their homes, cars, planes and offices.
5. Correct
6. Correct
7. Janet Brock, who has never missed a day of work, was promoted yesterday.
8. Correct
9. This desk, which was purchased in 1952, is Mr. Dooley's pride and joy.
10. Correct

SEMICOLONS

1. office;
2. equipment;
3. party;
4. notices;
5. known;
6. service;
7. department;
8. security;
9. serious;
10. choices;
11. work;
12. promoted;
13. elevator;
14. party;
15. deadline;
16. vacation;
17. responsibilities;
18. Correct
19. Correct

COLONS

1. Correct 2. years:* 3. advice:* 4. district: 5. vote:† 6. office:* 7. service: 8. supplies: 9. booming: 10. Correct

DASHES

1. month—unless
2. Correct
3. computer—the XR70—can
4. firm—brand-new
5. you—and I'm glad I'm not—I'd
6. employees—clerks included—are
7. examples—all
8. stop—I've
9. continues—and there is no reason why it should not—we
10. plan—you

APOSTROPHES

1. Frank's
2. Friday's, Jones's
3. assistant's, lawyers', attorneys'
4. Dawson's, Region's
5. Jim's, office's
6. women's, men's
7. machine's
8. man's, women's
9. Sarah's, Dawn's
10. XR70's, 3200's

*A colon is not the only acceptable solution here. See the section on dashes.
†A semicolon may also be used, instead of a colon.

APPENDIX B
Fry's Readability Graph

FRY'S READABILITY GRAPH

Take a letter or memo you've written recently, and score it according to the following "Graph for Estimating Readability," by Edward Fry, Ph.D., Director, Reading Center of Rutgers University.

Directions:

1. Randomly select three (3) sample passages and count out exactly 100 words each, beginning with the beginning of a sentence. Do count proper nouns, initializations, and numerals.
2. Count the number of sentences in the hundred words, estimating the length of the fraction of the last sentence to the nearest one-tenth.
3. Count the total number of syllables in the 100-word passage. If you don't have a hand counter available, an easy way is to simply put a mark above every syllable over one in each word, then when you get to the end of the passage, count the number of marks and add 100. Some calculators can also be used as counters by pushing numeral 1, then pushing the + sign for each word or syllable when counting.
4. Enter graph with number of sentences and *average* number of syllables; plot dot where the two lines intersect. Area where dot is plotted will give you the approximate grade level.
5. If great variability is found in syllable count or sentence count, putting more samples into the average is desirable.
6. A word is defined as a group of symbols with a space on either side; thus *Joe, JRA, 1945,* and *&* are each one word.
7. A syllable is defined as a phonetic syllable. Generally, there are as many syllables as vowel sounds. For example, *stopped* is one syllable and *wanted* is two syllables. When counting syllables for numerals and initializations, count one syllable for each symbol. For example, *1945* is four syllables, *IRA* is three syllables, and *&* is one syllable.

Remember, readability measurements are always rather rough approximations. It's an inexact science. Measuring merely one sample is not enough; it's better to consider the results of at least three samples averaged together. When textbook editors rate a book, they assess samples from each chapter before arriving at a final averaged readability level.

GRAPH FOR ESTIMATING READABILITY

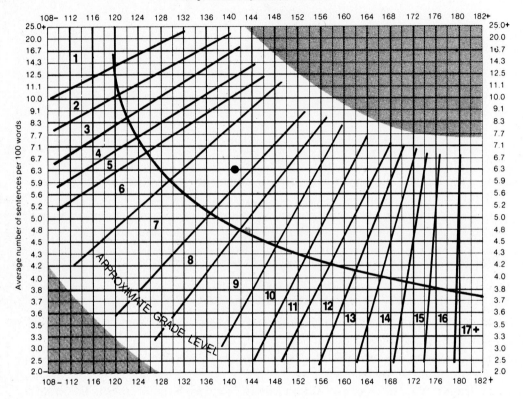

Average number of syllables per 100 words

SUGGESTED READING

Barnet, Sylvan, and Stubbs, Marcia. *Barnet & Stubbs's Practical Guide to Writing.* Boston: Little, Brown & Company, 1975.

*Blumenthal, Joseph C. *English 3200,* 3d ed. New York: Harcourt Brace Jovanovich, 1981.

*Brusaw, Charles T.; Alred, Gerald J.; and Oliu, Walter E. *The Business Writer's Handbook.* New York: St. Martin's Press, 1977.

Elbow, Peter. *Writing with Power.* New York: Oxford University Press, 1981.

*Ewing, David. *Writing for Results.* New York: John Wiley & Sons, 1974.

Holcombe, Marya W., and Stein, Judith K. *Writing for Decision Makers.* Belmont, Cal.: Wadsworth Publishing Co., 1981.

*Hopper, Vincent F., and Gale, Cedric. *Practice for Effective Writing.* Woodbury, N.Y.: Barron's Educational Series, 1971.

Laird, Dugan. *Writing for Results.* Reading, Mass.: Addison-Wesley Publishing Co., 1978.

Miller, Casey, and Swift, Kate. *The Handbook of Nonsexist Writing.* New York: Harper & Row, 1980.

Roman, Kenneth, and Raphaelson, Joel. *Writing That Works.* New York: Harper & Row, 1981.

Shaw, Fran Weber. *30 Ways to Help You Write.* New York: Bantam Books, 1980.

Tichy, H. J. *Effective Writing for Engineers, Managers, Scientists.* New York: John Wiley & Sons, 1966.

Zinsser, William. *On Writing Well,* 2d rev. ed. New York: Harper & Row, 1980.

*Especially recommended because they contain excellent practice drills and exercises in addition to information.

ABOUT THE AUTHOR

Deborah Dumaine is the founder of Better Communications, a firm that specializes in improving executive communication skills. Ms. Dumaine holds graduate and undergraduate degrees from Smith College and also teaches organization communications at the Simmons Graduate School of Management. She lives in Boston and in Martha's Vineyard.